To Fay,

Keep _____

_____

11/18/95

To Fay —
   Thanks for your
Kindness, example +
friendship. Enjoy the book!
            Ronda
            11/18/95

We Weren't Poor--
We Just Didn't Have
Any Money

We Weren't Poor — We Just Didn't Have Any Money

Carl Hurley

Cowcumber Books

McKinney Associates, Inc.
P. O. Box 5162
Louisville, KY 40255-0162

Printed in the United States of America

Library of Congress Cataloging-in-Publication Data

Application in progress

To my friends and kinfolks in the Appalachian Mountains, who taught me to see the humor in life.

Contents

A tribute
(ordinarily called the Foreword, but why be ordinary?)

How would you define *fun*?

One of my definitions is "Carl Hurley, laughmaker supreme."

Carl makes me laugh when I need to laugh . . . he makes me think. Best of all, he brings me memories of things I need to remember:

* like hard work and the valuable lessons it taught me;

* like "make-do" when there wasn't any other way;

* like the plain-vanilla saints who blessed me;

* like certain characters in my recall who taught me a lot about "how-not-to."

Being a minister, I appreciate Carl's pictures of the early church and its positive influence. I also go big for his emphasis on home life and family . . . and, in a world like ours, I'm glad

Carl lives by the old-time adage:

> "If you can't be funny and clean,
> then just be clean."

Carl, you make me glad the Good Lord invented me with a funnybone.

I hope *We Weren't Poor—We Just Didn't Have Any Money* sells and sells to bless and bless.

In appreciation,

Charlie Shedd

"Is there anything more precious to you than your memories? Good memories of days gone by are among our greatest riches."

We just didn't have any money

I GREW UP IN THE FOOTHILLS of the Appalachian Mountains in the '40s and '50s. We lived very much like people had for decades — close to the land. Grew almost all our own food. Wore homemade clothes. Spending money was a rarity. Most people didn't have electricity or an automobile. The Great Depression had ended some time back, but we didn't get word of it. Not for years. So we went on living the way we'd always lived.

Most homes didn't have central heat. They didn't have running water either, or inside plumbing. I've heard Uncle Arlo laugh and say many times, "You couldn't find ten dollars in this whole community. Not if you used the High Sheriff with a pocketful of search warrants."

But if you'd said we were poor, we'd have been highly insulted. We weren't poor — we just didn't have any money.

5

Being short of cash is one thing. Being poor goes beyond not having money. Being poor means you don't have the necessities; life is a struggle day to day. Being poor means there's little hope for a better future. Sometimes it means your relationships are more of a burden than a blessing.

No, we didn't have any money, but we were rich in the things that really matter.

When my little sister Norma Jean and I would come home from school, there was always a good supper on the table. We never worried about our next meal. Mama and Dad were always there. We never had to wonder if we were loved. Both sets of grandparents lived close by. Plus we had enough aunts, uncles and cousins to fill a football stadium. We were a close family.

Our parents worked hard, and they expected us to work hard, too. We went to church on Sunday. They taught us right from wrong and how to live by the Golden Rule.

We lived in a modest little frame house that had a front porch with a swing. The whole house had been built by our father with the help of a few neighbors. Nothing fancy, but it was a home filled with love. Like yours, my home contained some of the greatest memories of my childhood.

Is there anything more precious to you than your memories? Good memories of days gone by are among our greatest riches. That's what this book is about. Memories.

As you'll soon discover, my memory is so good it may go a little beyond what actually happened. Don't be concerned. Every story falls into one of three categories:

It happened that way.

It happened somewhat that way.

It could have happened that way.

I've always said there are times when facts shouldn't get in the way of a good story. And sometimes I've changed the names so I can still attend family reunions.

Our journey will take you on the backroads of my mind, and I hope you enjoy the trip. We'll visit some friends and kinfolks, sit on the front porch, sip sweet tea and take a swim in the creek. I'll introduce you to a bundle of colorful characters. We'll relive some customs of the mountains and reminisce about how things used to be.

I hope our sojourn brings back some of your favorite memories, too.

There are two great things about mind trips — you always arrive on time and there's no lost luggage. So pack your bag and get ready to travel. Don't bring anything fancy — we're just family. No ritzy hotels or gourmet restaurants along the way. But don't you worry. My kinfolks have always had an extra bed and plenty home cooking on the table. Remember, we weren't poor — we just didn't have any money.

"Ole Maude (she was our family horse) must have known something was up. She'd never been saddled that early in the morning. So off she went, breath billowing from her nostrils."

A ten-dollar package

"IT'S TIME FOR YOU TO CALL THE DOCTOR, honey." (Mama whispering, trying not to show her anxiety.)

Dad jumps out of bed, house icy cold. Whose fault was that? Dad's. Knowing the event was near, he'd been so excited the night before, he'd forgot the stove. Always banked it before bedtime.

It was a typical winter day. Snow covering the ground, fierce wind howling through the pine trees.

Didn't have a telephone. Few people did, so the nearest one was several miles away.

Must have been some sight. Dad. Building a fire to get the house warm. Grabbing his warmest clothes, scrambling to the barn, dressing as he went.

Ole Maude (she was our family horse) must have known something was up. She'd never been saddled that early in the morning. So off she went, breath billowing from her nostrils. She hit her stride and never looked back.

Most telephones were wooden boxes back then. Wooden boxes mounted on the wall, mouthpiece in front, crank on the side. Dad reached the operator and placed his call.

"Git here as quick as you can," he begged.

Have you guessed what was causing this excitement?

Me.

Carl Edward on the way. Carl Edward was arriving.

You picked a bad morning, Carl Edward. But they didn't fuss at me.

It was March 23, 1941. And who could fuss on March 23 when Carl Edward arrived?

By the time Ole Maude got back home, I'd already met my mama. Can you imagine what it was like for her, giving birth without a doctor? Mountain women are known for being strong, and my mama was no exception. She liked me right away, and so did my dad. Wadn't that nice?

The doctor?

One hour later, here he came in his old Model A Ford. Dad met him on the front porch.

"Both in there, waitin' for you, Doc."

"Got here as fast as I could. Long way from town in this kind of snow."

"No complaint, Doc. Believe me, no complaint."

Not from the doctor, either, when he checked

me, then Mama. Said we both looked good, considering.

On his way out the door, the doctor turned to Dad. "That'll be ten dollars for the house call."

"Ten dollars!" That was big money for Dad.

Of course, I don't remember any of this myself. But you can count on it—every word was just like my dad told it to me. Many, many times he told it to me.

He loved to tell it to me, and I loved to hear it.

I even liked it when he'd say with a wink, "Look at you. Sure got cheated that morning, didn't I? Ten dollars for a doctor, and you already here."

"You had to be careful sliding over if someone came to join you. A nail head hooked in the seat of your pants could leave part of your Sunday best right in the pew."

Show business,
here I come!

WHEN PEOPLE ASK ME HOW LONG I'VE BEEN GOING TO CHURCH, I say, "My mama started taking me before I was born."

That's the truth.

Our little church, Mt. Zion Baptist, was located down over the hill. It was less than a mile from our house, and we were there every time the doors opened.

It wasn't much to look at. A one-room, weatherboarded building with homemade furniture. Even the altar looked old and worn. The pews were made from wood strips about three inches wide, so watch out. With big spaces in between, sometimes the nails would work up from the seats. You had to be careful sliding over if someone came to join you. A nail head hooked in the seat of your pants could leave part of your Sunday best right in the pew. It might even leave some of your anatomy with it.

No, the building wasn't a majestic temple, but it served us well. Membership was made up largely of my family, both sets of grandparents, plus a gaggle of aunts, uncles and cousins. The rest of the congregation were close friends and neighbors.

Other than the people, could you guess what I remember most? It was all those wonderful Sunday School programs. Especially one that had a profound influence on my life.

I was five years old.

Every child in our class was asked to go to the front of the church and give a speech. We could tell a story from the Bible or recite some verses that we'd learned in class. Our teacher sat us together in the "amen corner." (That meant seats alongside the pulpit.) We were dressed in our very best, and the church was packed with family members.

The program started. Up we went, one by one. Some of the little kids forgot their lines. Others recited as fast as they could and rushed back to their seats. The audience was sympathetic. None of us was old enough to read.

When they called my name, I walked to the front of the pulpit and looked at the crowd. First time ever for me. I felt a tingle of excitement and took a deep breath. In my best stage voice, I told the crowd how "Jesus fed the multitude with three fishes and five loaves of light bread."

The audience roared. I didn't know why, but I liked it. It was a great feeling making people laugh.

What was so funny? Guess it was that "light" bread. You see, I only knew about three kinds of bread. Mama made biscuits and corn bread, and we bought light bread from the grocery. Called it "light" because of its texture, and it always came in loaves. Stood to reason, if Jesus used loaves, they had to be that "light" kind we ate at home.

In the years that followed, I thought a lot about that program. I didn't know it at the time, but it provided the first indication of all the fun I'd have with "light" humor. Interesting, isn't it, how one Scripture can change your life?

"I thought I'd invented a fine new way for milking cows on cold days."

The cow that jumped
over the moon

WHEN I WAS GROWING UP ON THE FARM, everyone had chores. We never gave it much thought; we just did them. That was our way of life.

After supper it was my duty to feed the hogs and chickens. Then I'd get in coal for the fire and draw water from the well. We didn't have a pump. Instead, we got our water by lowering a pail into the well. Drawing up one bucket at a time was not a fun job.

I seldom forgot to draw water, but if I did, Mama had a way of getting my attention. She'd roust me out of my cozy bed before daylight, and off I'd go to the well. Cold. Cold. Cold.

When it was that cold, the rope froze to its pulley. Getting it unstuck improved my memory for sure.

I started milking cows when I was so little I didn't need a milk stool. Standing straight up, I'd be exactly the right height to milk Ole Nell.

Ole Nell was our gentle milk cow. Slow moving. Good natured. She didn't give a lot of milk, but we were welcome to what she had. Ole Nell was one gracious old lady.

One morning, after I'd finished the rest of my chores, it was Ole Nell's turn. I got my bucket and stool and was ready to commence milking. Snow was flying, and the wind whistled through the cracks of our barn.

Even though I was bundled up in my warmest clothes, I was still cold. My hands especially, even in a pair of coarse-textured work gloves. I knew I should take off those gloves. But, I was convinced if I did, my hands would freeze to the bone.

Ole Nell didn't notice at first. She was busy eating. I thought I'd invented a fine new way for milking cows on cold days. Then, suddenly, Ole Nell felt something unexpectedly rough on her udder. What she felt was scratchy gloves where hands usually soothed.

You guessed it. Suddenly, Ole Nell became not-so-gentle. She popped her head out of the feed box, looking at me with eyes as big as saucers. Loudest bawling I ever heard. Here came the kick of Ole Nell's life. At which moment, I went one way, the milk bucket went the other way, and the milk went every which way.

One day when my little sister was reading from her story book, she exclaimed, "Carl, did you know cows can jump over the moon?"

Did I know, my dear Norma Jean? I was there when it happened.

"At the start of school, we each brought a drinking cup from home. Then, at the end of the year, we took 'em home for a good washing."

School days

Advice from a humble humorist:
Don't let your favorite memories get away from you.

A favorite memory of mine is starting school. I'm sure it's a day you remember, too.

Mt. Zion Elementary was almost two miles from our house. Only one room, but plenty big for only twelve students.

Off we went, Mama and I, hand-in-hand. Little Carl, age seven, scrubbed. Wide-eyed, ready.

When we entered the room, my first impression was the smell. Did your school have a particular aroma? Mt. Zion's was a combination of chalk dust, oil from the wooden floor and resin from the pine walls. I stood for a few minutes, smelling up the surroundings. Somewhat pleasant blend, really. My smeller has always been one of my strong points. If the scents were this inviting, I might do just fine here.

The room had four rows of seats in different sizes. Small ones in the front; large ones in back. The kids were different sizes, too. A potbellied stove sat in the middle of the room (to give equal-opportunity heat, I suppose). There was a recitation bench up front by the teacher's desk, and a chalkboard covered the front wall.

Shelves in the back, lots of shelves. That's where we put our lunch pails. This was long before school cafeterias, so what we ate we brought from home. Back there by the door stood a stand for the water bucket. Water was carried from the farmhouse down the road.

At the start of school, we each brought a drinking cup from home. Then, at the end of the year, we took 'em home for a good washing.

There, in the corner, see that worn-looking basketball, softball and bat? I'd heard my older friends talk about recess, and, without exception, they said it was a lot of fun.

Slowly, I eased into one of the little desk seats.

When I glanced back, Mama was gone, and the teacher started to talk. I don't remember one thing she said that day; I was too fascinated with my surroundings.

And why not? This place, and everything in it, would be my center of concentration for the next five and a half years.

Did you start school in first grade? Our first year was called the "primer." Why? I suppose because it primed you for the first grade. Maybe it was because those days would prime you for life.

During the primer, we had three main subjects. Reading, writing and counting. I already knew my ABCs. I could count to one hundred, eyes closed. Mama had thoroughly primed me even before I started to school.

I loved reading from the little soft-back book they furnished. (We didn't get hard-back readers until the first grade.) I remember that little book till yet, some of it, by heart.

This is Alice.
This is Jerry.
This is Jip.
See Alice run.
See Jerry run.
See Alice and Jerry run.
See Jip run.
Run, Jip, run.

I still remember, too, what I thought the first time I read that book. "This is the runningest bunch I ever heard of."

Big change ahead. Mid-way through my fifth-grade year at Mt. Zion, Mama and Dad announced that we'd be changing schools. Mt. Zion was closing down; Norma Jean and I would be going to a new school.

Hazel Green, ten miles away, twelve grades. More things to learn. More years to learn them in. Excited? Yes. Nervous? Yes.

Right from the start, we'd ride a bus to the new school. We'd never even seen inside a school bus.

That yellow bus looked huge next morning when it came to a stop and we got on. We climbed aboard to a big "Howdy" from the driver. "Howdy," we said back. For the next seven and a half years, we'd be greeted by the same "Howdy." For the next seven and a half years, we'd "Howdy" back. (Things don't change much in the mountains.)

Norma Jean found a seat beside a girl she knew from church. I slid in beside a boy named Tommy. As we rode along the gravel road, we talked about knives, marbles, teachers; other knowns and unknowns. That kind of talk makes you friends real quick.

At last the bus eased onto a gravel parking lot, and we all got off. Those school grounds looked big, big; inside, big, big, too.

This was the longest corridor I'd ever seen. How long? Seemed like miles and miles. Miles and miles of kids, too. All together, this was another scene I'd remember forever. When your life changes, you don't forget it, do you?

"Class," the new teacher began, "we have a new student today. His name is Carl Hurley, and, of course, we're glad to have him in our class." Embarrassed? Of course, I was. But wasn't it kind of nice, too? And this part was extra nice: she didn't ask me to say anything that day.

Every year you grow a little older, the old memories grow more meaningful, don't they? And why do we remember certain funnies as we sort through all that memory? Maybe the Good Lord meant that as a special gift for those times when we need a blessing.

Well, here among all that "first-day-newness" is one of my very favorites. Don't laugh now—this is real serious. What I remember most is the new name I got that day, and here's how I got it.

That night, when we got home, our Uncle Otis was there visitin'. Of course, the talk at supper was all about our new school and how we liked it. Uncle Otis listened big. Then, when there was pause enough to slip into the conversation, he said, "Did you know you have a new name now?

You're Bullfrogs. Both of you. Everybody who goes to Hazel Green is a Bullfrog. It's automatic."

Uncle Otis continued, "Well, I had a pet bullfrog once. Name was Waldo, and he was one tough bullfrog. Lived just about forever. Nicest pet I ever had. Real gentle, but tough, too. And he sure knew how to get out of the way. Anything come after him, he'd just jump one awful long jump. Then, he'd turn around and say real sassy, 'ribbet, ribbet, ribbet.'

"That's one of the school yells, and you'll be yelling it, too. Frog language: 'Ribbet, ribbet, ribbet.'

"Do you think it's stupid? Well, take it from your Uncle Otis, you could be something a lot worse than a bullfrog.

"TOUGH, BUT GENTLE. AND SMART ENOUGH TO GET OUT OF THE WAY WHEN YOU NEED TO."

Ribbet, ribbet, ribbet.

"I was never good at fighting. I thought it was stupid — maybe because I was small for my age and uncoordinated. I couldn't hit a bull on the backside with a bass fiddle."

The board of education

DID THEY WHIP CHILDREN AT YOUR SCHOOL? They sure did at mine.

Parents expected teachers to whip us when we needed it. We usually got it with a homemade paddle called "the board of education." Sometimes though, the teacher used a sourwood switch. And believe me, that hurt.

The quickest way to earn a good thrashing was for fighting. Interesting, don't you think? They hit us to teach us not to hit each other.

Fighting on the school ground was not uncommon. Somebody wearing a flashy shirt, carrying a lunch box too fancy — anything too different could bring on teasing. And as you might remember, teasing usually meant a fight.

I was never good at fighting. I thought it was stupid — maybe because I was small for my age and uncoordinated. I couldn't hit a bull on the backside with a bass fiddle.

One day my buddies Cletus Tussey and Murvin Rudy got into it during recess. A little first-grader ran inside and told the teacher they were fighting. Mrs. Ledford marched them back into the building, and the rest of us followed. An execution always draws a crowd.

So she took them to the front of the room and had them face us. There we sat, all big-eyed and very quiet.

The teacher turned to me. "Carl," she said, "Go get me a switch." A chill ran through me. "Oh, no," I thought. "I'd rather get the whipping myself than go for a switch." That would be like betraying my friends.

I looked at Cletus and Murvin. They understood the fix I was in. We were communicating without words. Just one look said, "You'd better not get a big one."

It wasn't uncommon for the teacher to send someone's friend after a switch. I dawdled. There she was saying it again, "Carl, I asked you to go get me a switch."

So off I went. In a few minutes I returned with the littlest possible switch. Not more than a foot long and about as big around as a pencil.

When I handed it to the teacher, she looked at me. "Carl," she said more firmly, "You go back and get me a big switch, and if it's not a really good one, I'm gonna get one myself and use it on *you*."

My buddies and I looked at each other again. They knew what I had to do. This time I brought in a sourwood switch about the size of a buggy whip. Murvin looked at me as though to say, "Didn't you overdo it?"

"This one will do fine," Mrs. Ledford said as I hurried to my seat.

Cletus and Murvin stood tall that day. They never cried. They took their punishment like a badge of honor.

But it was one of the funniest whippings I ever saw.

Cletus was wearing a brand-new pair of Duck Head overalls. The coarse blue denim was covered with a thick layer of dust from the schoolyard (he'd been fighting, remember?). As the teacher whopped him with that big switch, dust rolled up like she was beating a rug. Soon a brown haze hung over the room and all over the teacher.

When the dust cleared, justice had been dispensed. Poor teacher, though, she coughed all that afternoon, and, yes, all the next day, too. It broke our hearts.

Doesn't the Good Book say something like, "You get what's coming to you"?

"The place was a jungle sure enough. But way back there in the center was the most beautiful bicycle I ever saw."

The old, rusty bicycle

Do you remember your first bicycle? I'll never forget mine.

By the time I was old enough to say *bicycle*, I begged my daddy to get me one. Then something wonderful happened. I was almost ten, and we were at the hardware store. While Dad checked out the fishing tackle, I browsed through all those bicycles.

Twenty-five or thirty bicycles of different colors — they were something to see. Shiny chrome fenders, streamers hanging from handlebars, wire baskets, horns. A few even had luggage racks on the back. As I stood there drooling, a neighbor walked up.

"Gonna buy yourself a bicycle?" (Neighbor speaking.)

"Sure wish I could. Not enough money." (Me.)

Then, as the neighbor turned to leave, he paused, looked back at me and said one of the loveliest things I ever heard:

"You know? I've got an old bicycle. Belonged to my kids. But they're all moved off now, and I sure don't have any use for it. Needs a lot of fixin,' but I'll tell you what...I'd sell it to you for two dollars."

"Two dollars," I shouted. "I got that much saved up. I'll take it."

"It's a deal, kid. But first you talk to your dad. If he gives you the okay, stop by this morning and we'll do business."

When we pulled into the neighbor's driveway, he was there waiting for us. "Bike's around here behind the smokehouse, folks. Covered with horseweeds, probably, but I betcha we can find it."

And we did. The place was a jungle sure enough. But way back there in the center was the most beautiful bicycle I ever saw. Sure, it was covered with weeds...seat rotted away...chain broken...tires flat...some of the spokes out...but say it one more time — to me, absolutely beautiful.

Well, I looked at Dad, he looked at me, and then he said, "You and me together, son. We can make it beautiful again." On the way home, he added, "We'll send off to Sears Roebuck and get some parts. We'll fix it better than new, paint it your favorite colors, and just you see. Every kid in town will want one like it."

Seemed as if it took forever for those parts to come. But then one day when I got home from school, there was this big package leaning against our mailbox post. We spread out all the parts on our front porch, did an inventory and what a sight! Two tires, two tubes, two shiny chrome fenders, eleven spokes for the wheels and all kinds of other good stuff.

After supper Dad and I got the toolbox and went to work. Oh how we worked. Two days later we had my bicycle ready to ride. I'd painted the fenders glossy black, and you can believe with those chrome fenders, it was some sight. Honest, it looked better than the bikes in the Western Auto.

"Time to try her out," Dad said. So we pushed the bike to the driveway. Mama and Norma Jean came to watch. "Here I go," I shouted as I threw my leg over the seat.

I was never very big, and this was a big bicycle, so my feet barely reached the pedals. The bicycle wobbled like a newborn calf. Sure I fell a few times, but as my confidence grew, I picked up speed.

Now "burning the wind," as they called it, I headed for the barn. But wouldn't you know, speeding like crazy, my front wheel hit a rock. I swerved off the driveway straight into the chicken yard.

Off I went, and the next three things I remember were (a) all those chickens squawking like crazy, (b) my little sister shouting, "Ride 'em

35

cowboy," and (c) my mother wringing her apron and saying, "I'm going to the house before you kill yourself on that thing."

Of course I was okay in a few minutes, and off I went to show my friends. No real damage, not even to my pride. How could I be anything but proud on a bicycle like that?

Miles and miles of fun that bicycle gave me. Years and years taking me places. Pride too, and the satisfaction of owning something I'd rescued from a weed patch to make it beautiful again.

But don't you know there was one thing more, and this one lasted forever:

EVEN TODAY I'M THANKFUL FOR A DAD WHO CARED ENOUGH TO SAY, "SURE WE CAN REBUILD IT, SON. YOU AND ME TO-GETHER CAN MAKE IT BEAUTIFUL AGAIN."

"From the bag she took a handful of big, blunt-looking needles. There they lay in a neat little circle. By this time I was saying, 'Lord, if you will help me through this, I'll be a good boy for the rest of my life.'"

Terror in a white dress

Do you remember getting vaccinations at school?

Nowadays, parents take their kids to a doctor for inoculations. But when I was a boy, a nurse would make her rounds to all the one- and two-room schools in the county. She'd vaccinate us for all known diseases, plus a few that hadn't been discovered yet.

One year just after school started in the fall, someone whispered, "Here she comes." Heads turned. Necks stretched. We peered out the window as a solid black, humpback Chevrolet came around the curve. Dust from the gravel road rolled up behind it. Oh, mercy!

A large, red-haired woman got out of the car. Against the background of her white nurse's uniform, her black satchel looked as big as a suitcase. She walked across the yard, and here she was.

We all tried to look brave. Some of the bigger boys, eighth-graders, were as big as the teacher. They weren't afraid of man or beast. They would hunt, stay out all night with their coon dogs, run a bobcat up and down the riverbank. But with the arrival of the nurse, here came terror to their faces.

Everyone shuffled in their chairs. One boy tried to excuse himself. The teacher positioned herself by the door, and standing guard, she held a paddle. How big? Looked the size of a small ironing board. This encouraged everyone to stay put. No escape.

Now the nurse walked to the teacher's desk. She covered the desk with a big white cloth and began to unload her tools. Total silence in the room. She laid out a pile of cotton swabs, vials of vaccine and a large bottle of alcohol.

But the scariest thing was yet to come. From the bag she took a handful of big, blunt-looking needles. There they lay in a neat little circle. By this time I was saying, "Lord, if you will help me through this, I'll be a good boy for the rest of my life." Then she reached in and pulled out a large, metal instrument.

Looked the size of a grease gun. Had to be big to hold all the vaccine and the big, blunt needles.

Several of the little kids started to whimper. The bigger girls tried to comfort them, but everyone looked scared silly. Now big nurse stood up, smiling her wicked smile. "Well," she said, "who'd like to be first? Come on now, take this nice medicine so you won't get sick."

My buddy Murvin Rudy yelled, "I'd rather be sick."

Cletus Tussey, sitting behind Murvin, whacked him on the back of the head and said, "Get on up there — you're big and tough." Everyone laughed.

"Cletus," the nurse said, "why don't you come on first? You're big and tough, too."

Cletus turned as pale as a bedsheet. He locked his arms and legs around his desk and gave the nurse a determined look. "I ain't gonna take no shots this time," he said.

The teacher nodded to several big boys. Murvin, Burl and Larvel rose from their desks. They lifted Cletus, chair and all, and took him to the nurse. You can believe Cletus did get his shots.

One by one, the rest of us went forward. One by one, we gave in. Then the terror in a white dress packed up and said she'd see us next year. I'll never forget inoculation day and its wonderful ending. There we stood at the window and watched with relief as the taillights of the Chevrolet disappeared around the bend.

Then Cletus broke the silence with, "That old needle didn't hurt me none."

Everyone laughed.

Of course I know now it was a good thing that nurse was doing for us in the old school.

But isn't that the way it goes? So many of life's negatives turn into positives, don't they?

"First base was about fifteen feet from the biggest cliff. If you ran too far past first, you never made it to second. As you can imagine, it was especially dangerous for a visiting team."

Mattie at the bat

WHAT WAS YOUR FAVORITE SPORT growing up?

Softball was mine. I wasn't much good at it, but I sure liked softball.

When we played, the whole school got involved. Boy or girl, you could be on the team. I suppose there being only twelve students in our school had something to do with that.

Our games had a somewhat different twist.

The field was small. There was a gravel road on one side and a row of cliffs on the other. Home plate was under a big oak tree at the edge of the woods. First base was about fifteen feet from the biggest cliff. If you ran too far past first, you never made it to second. As you can imagine, it was especially dangerous for a visiting team.

Hit the ball over the cliff, and you had an automatic home run. When that happened, both teams would go up and over the cliff looking for the ball. No ball, no game. You can see why at

Mt. Zion Elementary, we called it "cliff softball."

I'll never forget one particular game. It was on a sunny afternoon in September, and we were playing Mt. Olive. There we were, standing under the shade trees having lunch, waiting for the enemy. Cleofus Johnson was a fifth-grader and one of our strongest hitters. He also had the loudest voice, and I loved to hear him holler, "Here they come!"

All heads turned to see that gaggle of strange kids coming down the road. One had a bat over his shoulder. Another was pitching a ball in the air. Walking fast, their heads bobbed like a herd of turtles.

Then all of us met at home plate. Our pitcher shook hands with their pitcher. Somebody yelled, "Play ball," and we did. Our teachers stood under a shade tree to watch and socialize.

Visiting teams always batted first. So one of their boys stepped up to the plate. His overalls were rolled to his knees, and he was barefoot. He tightened his galluses, pulled down his cap bill, took a practice swing and yelled, "Pitch it to me, baby."

It was one close game all the way.

Now came the last inning, score tied. Excitement at a fever pitch when we came to bat.

Mattie was up. She was a stout girl from one of our poorest families. You can bet, though, there wasn't anything poor about the way she hit that ball. Believe me, she could knock it farther than anyone we'd ever seen.

This day she wore a skirt about three sizes too big. Obviously somebody's hand-me-down. Top part wrapped around her waist and fastened with a big safety pin. Looked like somebody in her family might have been umpteen times bigger than she was. That monster garment reached to her ankles, but she came up proud.

You would've felt real confident the way Mattie grabbed that bat and twisted her hands around it. Looked like she was wringing out a pair of wet socks.

So there she stood, staring that pitcher straight in the eye.

"Slug it, Mattie!" "Show 'em what you got, Mattie." "You're our girl, Mattie." All kinds of cries rang out loud, loud, loud.

Then the Mt. Olive pitcher let loose a slow, lofty ball. Mattie took a half step into it and cracked that ball into deep left field. We cheered as Mattie started around the bases.

Then it happened. Half way between first and second, Mattie hooked her toe in that long skirt and ran slap-dab out of the thing. Everyone laughed, but Mattie never stopped. Safe on second, she laughed at her predicament. Then she pulled her sweater down as far as it would go and charged on unencumbered. When she got to third, one of the other girls fetched Mattie's skirt and helped her pin it back on. (As you can tell, the way she'd hit that ball, there was plenty of time.) Rigged up again, here she came. "Slide, Mattie, slide," we yelled. (They'd found the ball now.) So slide she did and scored the winning run.

You can see, can't you, why we all called it the funniest ballgame ever? But wasn't it one of the teachingest?

Thank you, Mattie. I bet everyone who saw you that day would say the same thing: "Don't let a little adversity keep you from winning the big game."

"The new mule wasn't used to riding in a truck. When we came through town, his eyes got as big as saucers, and his ears stuck straight up."

The pea-vine mule

GROWING UP ON A HILLSIDE FARM wasn't easy. Our food came mostly from the land. All of it was the product of hard work. And I mean really hard work by the whole family.

In the spring, we planted a large garden. We planted everything edible — anything you could can, anything you couldn't can but could dry, anything you couldn't can or dry but could preserve.

Mama stayed busy during the growing season "puttin' up" food. You can believe we ate well.

Farm tractors hadn't reached the Appalachian foothills yet. We'd seen pictures of them in *Progressive Farmer* magazine. But almost every family owned a good pair of mules.

And if not two, at least one good, gentle garden mule. *Gentle* included staying within the rows and not stepping on the vegetables.

Our mules were considered extensions of the

family. For instance, one day Uncle Arlo was plowing close to a cliff. Aunt Mavis hollered out the back door, "Y'all be careful out there. If you fall over that cliff and hurt my mule, I'll beat you like a country boy pickin' a banjo." (She probably wouldn't admit it, but I think down deep she was concerned about Uncle Arlo, too.)

One day, Dad came in the house and announced it was time to get a new mule.

"Why?" we asked.

"Ole Maude has gone into retirement. I just came from the barn. She's plowed her last row and okra-nibbled her last nubbin. She's gone to the big sweet-corn patch in the sky."

The next day, we loaded in our farm truck and headed to the livestock sale in London. I was excited. Sales day at the stockyard was a festive occasion. All kinds of interesting farm animals were sold. Plus lots of trading in knives, guns, hunting dogs, mules—almost anything. A good country auctioneer could keep the excitement going all day. The whole event was something like a county fair without the Ferris wheel. No cotton candy, either.

About mid-afternoon, we found the mule we'd been looking for. He was a little "pea-vine" mule. That's what people called mules that had a small build. We loaded him into the truck and headed for home. Dad gave me the job of keeping an eye on the mule to make sure he was riding okay.

The new mule wasn't used to riding in a truck. When we came through town, his eyes got as big as saucers, and his ears stuck straight up. We'd driven through London and were entering East Bernstadt.

One side of Main Street had a grocery, a hardware store and a few other buildings. The train depot was on the other side, and the train track ran right alongside the street.

Wouldn't you know, just as we rolled through the middle of town, here came a freight train. Black smoke rolling, steam flying out the side. I looked back. Our new mule was jumping, swishing his tail and kicking. Bellering, too.

"Stop the truck," I yelled. "That mule is trying to get out."

At that moment, the train blew its whistle. The mule reared on its hind legs just as Dad hit the brakes. The sudden stop flung the mule forward, out of the truck bed and right on top of the truck cab. We hopped out, wondering what to do. The mule just stood there, shaking, with a puzzled look on his face.

With the help of a few excited bystanders, we were able to get the mule back into the truck bed. We were lucky that no one, including the mule, was hurt that day.

We named our new mule Casey Jones in honor of the great train engineer. That mule worked out his days on our little hillside farm like

Ole Maude before him. Every time I go home to East Bernstadt and cross that railroad track, comes another wonderful recall from my boyhood. Somewhere, deep inside me, I hear a freight train blowing in memory of Casey Jones the Mule.

"There's never been a fatality at White Oak Creek, and that's amazing, really. Guess there must have been some kind of special angels looking over us boys."

My favorite swimming hole

IF YOU GREW UP IN THE COUNTRY, you probably have fond memories of a favorite swimming hole.

It might be a beautiful pool, a wide place in some creek, a neighbor's farm pond, or that beautiful river.

Great memories, aren't they? Skinny dipping on a Sunday afternoon. That big outing on July 4th. With so many rivers and streams, eastern Kentucky is full of swimming holes.

My favorite was White Oak Creek. About a mile and a half from our house, nestled between two hills, White Oak Creek had the only natural waterfall in our area. And was that ever fun? Anyone who has swung on a grapevine over a river will know what I mean. Swing out, farther, faster. If you've ever had that experience, if you've swung out belly first for a waterfall, you'll remember just how much fun it was.

On one side of White Oak Creek, there were large rocks jutting out. On the other, was a beautiful sand bar. Over the years, falling water had eroded the creek bottom there to make it deep, deep. Deep enough for diving. A small cliff on the hillside made a perfect place to jump. Run off the hill, bounce off the rock, tuck your knees against your chest, grasp your ankles and let yourself fall. We called this "shooting a cannonball." Big, big fun.

Summertime when the mountain laurel was blooming, it was also a great place to just sit. Natural beauty everywhere. Listen to the constant music of that falling water. Stress relief at its best. Beauty. Contentment. Pure peace.

Except for one day.

I'd just finished chopping weeds from our sweet corn patch. I'd also hoed a half-acre of potatoes. Now here I was at the end of the last row, and can you hear the car horn? My buddies: Cletus, Bobby Earle and Leroy. After all that work, I deserved a break, didn't I? So I pitched down the hoe, jumped the fence and we were off.

Cletus parked his car at the edge of the main

road, and we made our way down a little path.
"Man, this is really something!" Leroy speaking.
He was visiting from Detroit. "Never seen a
swimming hole like this, fellows."

Now Cletus had shucked his clothes and was
running over the hill. "Last one in is a rotten egg."
(First one in always yelled that gem of intelligence.)
Bobby Earle was right behind him. Me, I walked
farther down the path and waded in from the
sand bar. I preferred getting used to the water
gradually, but I also preferred the others scare off
those water snakes.

We splashed around a few minutes, throwing
water in each other's face, having a great time.
Leroy was still on the cliff, watching. "Come on
in," Cletus yelled. "Water's great." So Leroy
disappeared in the bushes. In a few minutes, he
came out wearing his store-bought bathing
suit. (Remember, he was from the city.)

Leroy didn't get a running start — he just
backed up three steps and jumped.

"Wait!" Cletus yelled. But Leroy couldn't wait.
He was already in mid-air. And we had forgotten
to tell him something important.

Submerged two feet underwater, there was a
large rock you'd hit if you didn't jump far enough
out. Of course, we'd all miss it. We were used to
it. But Leroy wasn't.

You can believe we were breathless as Leroy
went under. Feet first he hit that rock, a glancing

blow. Seconds passed. Then Leroy's head popped up and we all rushed to him.

"You hurt, Leroy? You okay?"

No answer. No answer at all for what seemed like hours, weeks, months. Then, glory be. He shook his addled head and said, "Ain't as deep as it looks, is it?"

You can hear us laugh, can't you? Just to hear him talking made us laugh. This was laughing for relief. This was a "Thank you, Lord" laugh. No tragedy.

If you're ever in our neighborhood and you'd like to swim in our spot, please feel welcome. But don't you forget. There's a big rock under the water on the near side of that cliff.

There's never been a fatality at White Oak Creek, and that's amazing, really. Guess there must have been some kind of special angels looking over us boys.

So y'all come, you hear? But this isn't too much to ask, is it? You be real sure you bring your own angel.

"Uncle Arlo didn't join the church until he was older. He had what some called a 'checkered past.'"

Who am I to pass judgment?

BAPTISMS ARE ALWAYS SPECIAL TIMES in any church, aren't they?

Well, "baptizings" were big social events in the Appalachian Mountains. In our community they usually were held on Sunday afternoon following our annual revival in the fall.

Our preachers called it the "cleansing and purifying of new believers through the ordinance of baptism." It was a big day for all of us. An opportunity to visit with friends and enjoy the scenic beauty. Mountain streams, rolling hillsides, God's handiwork at its best.

Whether in a river, creek or farm pond, a good baptizing hole must meet several criteria. It should be fairly easy for people to get to. Ample space for the congregation to stand. Water shallow at the edge but gradually deeper to allow for easy in and out. Water waist deep allows the minister to immerse the candidates. Then they can be led back to the bank with little difficulty.

Our little church has an indoor baptistry now, but not back then. This particular baptism I'm telling you about was performed at the swimming hole on White Oak Creek. No River Jordan this. The ceremony wasn't fancy, either. Yet it was every bit as meaningful to us as baptism in an elaborate church baptistry.

We sure had one thing going for us, though. The hills on each side formed an amphitheater. Those acoustics gave our singing a special quality. The melody rose above the slight roar of the waterfall, then drifted gently through the trees on the hillside. Even a nonbeliever would be touched by such music.

All these beautiful moments meant a lot to me. But some of them were plain funny. Like when they baptized Uncle Arlo.

Uncle Arlo didn't join the church until he was older. He had what some called a "checkered past."

There was a big crowd for Uncle Arlo's baptism. His was big-time "cleansing and purifying."

As I stood on the cliff watching the preacher put Uncle Arlo under, you couldn't guess what I heard. One of the "righteous sisters" said in a muted voice (but not so muted I didn't hear it), "One dunkin' ain't gonna do him no good. They'd better anchor him out in deep water and leave him out all night."

Now that wasn't real nice talk, was it? But watch it, Carl! What does the Bible say about judging?

"I can remember thinking, 'When I get big, I'm gonna join a church, all right, but my church will never meet on Saturday night.'"

The silver screen and Roy and Gene

GOING TO THE MOVIES is another fond memory of my childhood.

Saturday night. That was our night for the movies. Unless it was the first Saturday night of the month, that is. Our little church had its business meeting on the first Saturday night, with some preaching thrown in.

Mama and Dad believed if the church was in session, we should go there instead of anywhere else — even the movies. I can remember thinking, "When I get big, I'm gonna join a church, all right, but my church will never meet on Saturday night."

The Reda Theater was located on Main Street in London (London, Kentucky, you remember). Lights flashed on the marquee, and it was air-conditioned. Only place in town that was air-conditioned, except for the supermarket.

Weekends, there'd be a double feature—

usually a Western and some jungle movie. I liked them both.

Remember Jungle Jim? Tarzan was okay, but oh that Jungle Jim! He wore a khaki outfit (starched and pressed), a pith helmet and combat boots. Jungle Jim could dive in the river and swim four miles underwater with his boots on. He could even stab an alligator with his hunting knife and come up out of the river drier than a bone.

But my favorites were the Westerns. Roy Rogers and Gene Autry were great!

Once when I was old enough to go without my parents, Cletus and I hitched a ride to the Reda. My buddy Cletus lived back in the country farther than I did, and he'd never been to a movie.

We had saved up fifteen cents each for our tickets, ten cents for popcorn and one nickle for a "Co-Cola." So off we went.

When we entered the theater, Cletus felt air conditioning for the first time. He looked at me and said, "Man, it's cold enough in here to kill a hog." (We always did our butchering in the fall when it was cool enough. Why? So the meat wouldn't spoil.) We found our seats and settled down. Just as we dug into our popcorn, here came the Western on that big screen.

Cletus' eyes widened. He'd never seen any picture so big.

"Way off in the distance, Cletus, see that stagecoach? Now watch." Sure enough, as it got closer, a bunch of outlaws came riding from behind the rocks. Then, when they began shooting their pistols, would you believe? Cletus ducked down behind and a little bit under the seat in front of him.

"Get up," I said, "You're gonna miss the best part."

And I was right.

Suddenly, Roy arrived to search out the bad guys. They were hiding now behind another big rock, waiting to ambush Roy. Just as the meanest looking outlaw pulled his gun and aimed at Roy, Cletus jumped to his feet. "Hey," he yelled at the top of his voice. "Watch out! There's more of 'em behind the rocks." Everyone, except the usher, roared with laughter. Cletus kept quiet for the rest of the movie.

The Reda is gone now. A parking lot sits in its place. More modern theaters have taken over, and that's all right. Three cheers for progress. Yet Roy and Gene still ride the dusty trails in the backroads of my mind.

And that's okay, too, isn't it? Memory is one of the greatest gifts the Good Lord gave us.

" 'Look.' We did, and what do you think? Here came a little brown water snake heading straight for Effie Sue."

Shall we gather at the river?

WE HAD A SPECIAL REVIVAL in our little church one year. This one got going so strong it went into extra innings, like two weeks. How revivals were judged in those days depended on how many candidates for baptism they produced. Well, this one broke all the records. Fifteen people "came forward."

"A plentiful harvest" is what the visiting evangelist called it. So now came the baptizing. People drove from all over. My grandpa was the song leader, and he always picked the old-fashioned gospel hymns. This time it was "Shall We Gather at the River?"

Before the service, we'd warned the evangelist about our baptizing pond. White Oak Creek was shallow enough near the bank, but it gradually got deeper. Then fifteen feet out, the bottom dropped clean gone. All of a sudden the water was deep, deep.

That day as the preacher waded in, my buddies and I wondered. But, praises be, he stopped right there at the edge of that dropoff, exactly as we'd told him. Then he marked the spot with an upright stick. With that done, he went back to the bank and led the converts out. One by one he lined them up by the marker. So now he was ready for the immersions. (There was always a deacon on hand to lead them from the water. Very impressive.)

Two men were first, but next in line was Effie Sue Twiddle. Everyone held their breath now, because Effie Sue was one large woman. At least three hundred pounds worth.

This day Effie Sue was wearing a long, white dress, real big of course. Well, when she hit that water, her dress bulged out like a hot-air balloon. (She'd forgotten to tie that dress near the ankles.) Now I don't mean to be unkind, but from looking at her you'd know it had been a long time since she'd even seen her ankles. But baptized she would be, so some of the ladies helped her smooth the dress down and tie it tight. Then they helped her back into the creek.

Next? Well, just as the preacher positioned her for putting her under, one of my buddies said, "Look." We did, and what do you think? Here came a little brown water snake heading straight for Effie Sue. Of course she screamed, threw both hands up in the air and down she went. Naturally the preacher grabbed for her, and wouldn't you know — he fell backward into the water and down they went together. Plain disappeared.

Next a deacon tried to catch them both, but he lost his balance, and he was gone, too.

And here we all stood, stunned.

Seconds passed. The deacon surfaced first. Next Effie Sue's head popped up. Then came the preacher hanging on to Effie for dear life. Believe me, it was some sight, all three of them clutching each other the whole way back to bank.

Of course by now it was not exactly what you'd call an ideal setting for Holy Baptism. Not even a little bit Holy.

But I'll say this for that preacher. He turned Effie Sue around and led her straight back to water deep enough. Then, solemn as though nothing had happened, he baptized her real nice and dignified.

I'm sure you'll understand when I say, "All my life I've admired that man." I learned something that day about never give up no matter what.

So how did it all end? Would you believe this? After the somber part, that preacher gave us all a chance to laugh like total when he said, "Folks, when she grabbed me by the neck and fell on top of me in that deep water, I thought the Lord had called me home for sure."

Now that was some kind of man, wasn't it? And this is the thing I learned from him which has stayed with me to this day:

TURNING A NEAR DISASTER INTO ONE ROARING GOOD LAUGH MAY BE EXACTLY THE RIGHT PRESCRIPTION, IF IT'S DONE EXACTLY RIGHT!!!

"One little girl brought her doll to be Baby Jesus. Wrapped in a blanket and laid in the manger, with proper lighting from Larvel Atwell's kerosene lamp, it looked real lifelike."

Broadway can't top that

"FORTIETH AND PLUM" stood for forty miles from town and plumb back in the sticks. That's where our little community was at. (You're right. I probably should of said "was located.")

We were country folks. We spent more time looking at the south end of a northbound mule than attending cultural events. But we weren't hicks. We had culture just like they do in the big cities.

I'm talking about activities that went beyond an occasional quilting party. Beyond corn shucking, cane stripping or even footwashing at the Primitive Baptist church. I mean we had our own theatrical productions right there on the banks of the Rockcastle River. No, we didn't have great theaters like they have on Broadway. We didn't have a civic auditorium. But we did have the Mt. Zion church.

At least once a year we'd have a program. The church always produced a play at Christmas time.

Someone was selected to direct the program, and casting commenced.

It wasn't easy for those big, raw-boned country boys. But after some coaxing, they'd give in and accept a part. Then rehearsals would begin.

On Sundays we'd take a sack lunch, have a picnic and practice our play all afternoon. My grandmother was the director. As I look back, I'm not sure I even had a choice whether I'd be in the play. And it doesn't matter, because I loved it. To this day "play acting" is big on my list. As opening night grew closer, the rehearsals became more frequent, more intense. Frivolity was held to a minimum, and hard work took its place.

A small, one-room structure, the church didn't have an auditorium. So we had to create our own curtain. A few days before the play, volunteers would bring some baling wire and string. Then they'd stretch it across the front of the room. Eight or nine feet high, it ran from one side of the building to the other.

Next bedsheets were hung, and we had curtains. Sheets were also hung on each side of the stage to make a dressing area. Two people were selected to open and close the curtains before and after each act.

Props for the stage and costumes were a small problem, but we managed. There were no stores or costume houses where we could buy things like that. We had to make our own. One year, in preparation for the Christmas story, someone constructed a manger from saw mill slabs. Someone else brought a bale of straw. One little girl brought her doll to be Baby Jesus. Wrapped in a blanket and laid in the manger, with proper lighting from Larvel Atwell's kerosene lamp, it looked real lifelike.

Our neighbor Woodrow played Joseph. When he stepped on stage, he was wearing his wife's chenille robe. His turban was fashioned from a cotton bath towel. The audience tittered, but it didn't bother Woodrow. He stayed in character even though he looked more Woodrow than Joseph.

When he knocked on the inn door to say his piece, nothing came. He'd forgotten his lines. The innkeeper said, "Can I hep ye?" Woodrow froze and no words came.

But something did come from the audience — more giggles.

Then suddenly Woodrow knew what he was supposed to ask. "Y'all got airy room?"

Now the whole place erupted. The other actors erupted. The angels erupted. Even now I erupt when I think about it. But I get a real soft feeling in my heart when I remember thinking — even the baby Jesus seemed to smile.

Then the play was over. Once more the Christmas story had been told. Told by a wonderful bunch of home folks doing their best with what they had.

And isn't that exactly what they did that night in Bethlehem?

"On Christmas Eve, we'd sit around the fireplace waiting for Santa Claus. Sometimes I was sure I caught a glimpse of his white beard at the window. Of course, the flickering lights helped that idea along."

Christmas in the country

HOW OLD WERE YOU when you quit believing in Santa Claus? I was nineteen. Looking back, it seems a bit old, doesn't it? But there was a reason. I simply couldn't believe my parents could afford all those presents under the tree.

Christmas was a special celebration. You could smell it coming. Ah, those aromas.

Mama baked sugar cookies shaped like stars and Christmas trees. And could she ever bake cakes! Jam cake with caramel icing. Fruit cakes so full of fruit, nuts and gumdrops they weighed twelve pounds! (Well, they seemed that heavy.)

Closer to Christmas Eve, she made candy. Peanut butter...peanut brittle...chocolate fudge with peanuts.

Divinity. And the sweet she called "sea foam." This one was made with egg whites and sugar.

During the holidays, we had to take turns sitting on the front porch. We got so fat the whole family couldn't fit inside the house at one time.

Then there was fruit. Our little store way out in the country didn't have fresh fruit real often. This made fruit a special treat. So every Christmas Dad bought a big bag of Florida oranges and a bushel of Washington apples. And apples baking have a special aroma, too! Oh, my.

Christmas smells. Supreme. Super. Elegant.

Yet fruits and their aroma weren't the only traditions.

Another was that our parents would take us kids to town for a special shopping spree. They'd give me and Norma Jean a dollar apiece. Big, big money. Then they'd turn us loose. We could buy anything we wanted as long as the money lasted. A dollar won't get you much today, but if you're as old as I am, you'll remember. Back then, it got us kids all kinds of things, didn't it? Comic books; coloring books; crayons; a small toy airplane. And even those wonderful things called Bob-Jacks.

Remember Bob-Jacks?

Jacks are funny little metal pieces with prongs going in every direction. A set of jacks comes with a small rubber ball. First, you'd throw the ball in the air. Then you'd see how many jacks you could pick up and still catch the ball on the first bounce.

Norma Jean always bought jacks at Christmas. She was real good at it, too. Beat me every time.

Another tradition was getting the tree. We lived close to the woods, and there were plenty of trees. We were choosy, so it took a while to get the right one. When we got it home, we'd make a base, set the tree in a corner of the living room and decorate it.

I always thought our tree was the prettiest and best decorated of anybody's. Some of our ornaments were regular old friends. You know what I mean? It wouldn't be *your* tree without those friendly old ornaments, would it?

On Christmas Eve, we'd sit around the fireplace waiting for Santa Claus. Sometimes I was sure I caught a glimpse of his white beard at the window. Of course, the flickering lights helped that idea along.

Before we went to bed, we'd get our stockings ready. I tied mine to the foot of the bed. That way, if I woke up during the night, I could check to see if Santa had arrived.

Then came the big moment. First thing when I woke up, I'd peek over the foot of the bed and see that long stocking filled to the brimming top. Apples. Oranges. Candy. Cracker Jacks. Nuts. Bubble gum. And always that big stick of red-and-white peppermint candy, right there on top looking me straight in the eye.

I was glad when nylon stockings made their way to our area. They stretched and could hold more. I can't help wondering what it would have been like if we'd had panty hose back in those days.

You can bet I was the first one up on Christmas morning. I'd slip into the living room to see if Santa had arrived. Do you remember some of the things you saw first on Christmas morning? The glimmer of the handlebars of your brand-new tricycle. That wonderful new sleigh. Memories you'll never forget, will you? And I won't, either.

I'd run to Mama and Dad's bedroom, yelling, "Come, see what Santa brung us." Then, I'd wake Norma Jean. Mama and Dad would follow us to the tree, poke up the fire and we'd celebrate (at something like four in the morning!).

I realize now how fortunate we were to have such good Christmases, even though money was scarce.

Aren't there times, on Christmas Eve, when you still catch a glimpse of a white beard in the window? And if your parents were like mine, you'll know what I mean when I say this:

WEREN'T WE FORTUNATE TO HAVE PARENTS WHO TAUGHT US THE DEEPER MEANING OF CHRISTMAS?

"For some reason, I had opened my eyes during the prayer. Maybe it was because I felt something unusual coming."

Not an atheist
in sight

LAST YEAR, Mama and I went back to Mt. Zion Baptist Church. That's where she took me when I was growing up.

The church has sure changed a lot. When I was a boy, it was weatherboard construction. Now, it's a beautiful red-brick building with store-bought pews. Carpet, too. There's even a baptistry behind the pulpit now, with a painted scene of the River Jordan as a backdrop. Quite a change from our baptizing hole on White Oak Creek.

The people have changed, too. Most of the older faces are gone. Some of the younger ones I knew as friends look exactly like their parents did when I was a teenager.

As I sat with Mama, my mind harked back to those Sunday mornings of my boyhood. When I closed my eyes, I could hear voices ring out the hymns: "The Old Rugged Cross," "Precious Memories," "Just As I Am."

Then as I mused, I remembered one particular Sunday morning.

That Sunday long ago, we'd finished some of those favorite hymns. The preacher was dangling us over hellfire (his speciality was "believe it or burn" sermons). For some reason, I had opened my eyes during the prayer. Maybe it was because I felt something unusual coming. Anyway, I noticed the room was getting darker. Too dark, really. I peeked out the window. I knew something fierce was on its way. Trees and bushes were twisting. The sky was getting blacker.

Then Dad leaned over and whispered, "This ain't no little springtime thunderstorm. This is a full-blown tornado."

Rain began to beat in torrents against the windows. Walls popped and cracked. The whole building shook. We huddled together in the center of the room.

The front wall broke loose, plumb loose. Would it cave in? Sure looked like it.

Then, suddenly, the storm went away just as swiftly as it had come.

Have you ever been through a storm like that? If you have, I know you'll understand what my dad said afterward. "No one killed. No one hurt. You know what I think? I think if anyone was behind in his praying, he sure got caught up today. Fact is, when that wall started to give, I looked around. I can guarantee you, there wasn't an atheist in sight. Not one!"

What really matters

I<small>T'S</small> <small>REFRESHING TO SEE THAT OUR LITTLE CHURCH</small> hasn't changed in the verities that really matter.

It still teaches right from wrong.

It still teaches the kind of love that accepts people as they are.

It teaches us to lend a helping hand to bless our friends and neighbors when they need it.

I hope these things never change in my little church.

You hope that for your church, don't you?

91

"Lightning flashed in the distance. Then, a mighty roll of thunder. What could we do? We just hoed faster."

Have hoe, will travel

AT THE END OF THE SCHOOL YEAR ONE SUMMER, my cousin Eldean and I needed some money. So we decided to start our own business.

Deciding what kind of business wasn't easy.

We'd sold subscriptions for the old-time magazine, *Grit*. We'd sold garden seeds door-to-door. Newspapers, too. Rosebud salve. Cloverine salve. And a bunch of other salves. But no matter how hard we tried, it always turned out the same. By the time we paid for the product and had a Moonpie apiece for lunch, we were pretty much back were we started.

What could we do? What kind of service did people need?

"I got it," Eldean said.

"Got what?" I replied.

"I know exactly how we can make some money."

"Tell me."

"Let's be gardeners."

"Great idea, Eldean."

We'd lived in the country most of our lives and worked in gardens since we were big enough to crawl. Of course, we knew all about chopping weeds, planting seeds and hoeing corn.

That night, we filed our garden hoes to a fine edge.

Early the next morning, Eldean and I headed down the road. Hoes over our shoulders, we were set for work.

First, we stopped at "Miss Mae's." Miss Mae was a widow who lived in a big, white farmhouse and had a large garden and corn patch.

"I sure *could* use some help," she told us. "The weeds are about to take over my sweet corn. When can you start?"

"Right now," we said.

"That's fine, 'cause it looks like rain, and I'd like to get those weeds chopped before it comes."

Off we went to her garden patch to show her what we could do. But in a few minutes, we noticed the sky was getting darker. Lightning flashed in the distance. Then, a mighty roll of thunder. What could we do? We just hoed faster.

"Ain't real close yet," Eldean cajoled. "We just got these two rows we're on, and two more. Maybe we can make it." We kept hoeing.

All at once, lightning flashed. The thunder was so loud it rattled the fillings in our teeth. Big drops of rain began to pepper the field.

"Let's get outta here," I yelled.

Eldean dropped his hoe and started to run. I followed, about fifty feet behind.

As Eldean cleared the patch, lightning struck closer, and he looked back. Just as he did, he stepped on a rake that had been left in the grass.

The handle flew up, hit him on the head, and knocked him colder than a kraut cellar.

I ran to him. Eldean was trying to sit up, but was considerably addled. I threw his arm over my shoulder and pulled him to the porch. Miss Mae brought a washcloth soaked in cold water. "Hold this on his head," she said. "He took quite a thumping there." I held the cloth to his forehead, and Eldean didn't say a word.

"My goodness," Miss Mae exclaimed. "That rake handle put a knot on your head the size of a hen egg." By now, Eldean had come to enough that he was holding the cloth himself. With a puzzled look, he said, "What rake handle you talking about?"

"The one you stepped on...the one that flew up and knocked you out." (Miss Mae.)

"Good Lordy, I thought lightning struck me." (Eldean.)

You know how you laugh like crazy sometimes when you've been so scared? Well, that's what we did. We laughed like crazy.

Miss Mae brought us some big glasses of sweet tea now. Some cookies, too. (She was famous for her cookies.)

There we sat on her back porch, watching the rain. Of course, when it stopped, the ground was too wet to finish the garden.

"We'll be back to finish when the ground dries," I said. Eldean added, "Provided it don't look like rain, and there ain't no lightning."

"I like work myself, but I rather put in with my cousin Eldean. He says work was invented for folks who don't like to fish."

The homemade
tractor

YOU HAVE SOME ANCESTORS YOU'RE REAL PROUD
OF, don't you? They're the kind who give you
confidence in yourself when you're a little bit
unsure. Nothing like a bit of inspiration straight
from the home folks, is there?

One person I love to recall is my dad and
how he did the best he could with whatever he
could afford. My dad was pure homespun inventor.
I don't know anything he ever got patented, but
you'd have been awed the way he "figgered on
things." That was his term for making do.
Sometimes he'd even create his own tools, which
he called "my homemade gadgets."

Dad never tried to get out of work. He loved
it. Me? I like work myself, but I rather put in with
my cousin Eldean. He says work was invented for
folks who don't like to fish.

One night at supper, Dad announced he
was going to build a tractor. "With all the plowin'

and farm chorin,' we shore need one." At that time there was only one tractor in the entire community. Most people farmed with horses and mules.

Well, when he said he was going to build a tractor, I thought, "This'll be something to see."

Me: "What you gonna build it from, Dad?"

Dad: "There's a fellow down the road, he's got an old car. I'm gonna buy it from him and turn it into a tractor."

Later that week the old car rolled into our driveway. I thought it was company coming till I saw Dad behind the wheel. He jumped out, slapped the fender and said, "What'cha think of her?"

"Sure looks like a tractor to me," I said.

So Dad gathered his tools, and we went to work. In two days we had her stripped down to nothing but engine, chassis and wheels. Next we added a truck transmission for power. Then we cut off the drive shaft to move the rear end forward. Why? So she could make the sharp turns tractors need to make.

Well, she sure did look funny, especially when we put those truck tires on her back wheels and some little car wheels up front. You'd have laughed out loud. Even sitting still, she looked like she was running downhill.

Now what would we do for a seat? Well, we took one from an old hay rake. Made from sheet metal, it had little round holes (about the size of a quarter) all over it to let the rainwater through. So with the seat fastened in place, we were ready to go.

As we stood admiring our work, a neighbor walked up. He'd heard about our project and wanted to see it. Dad said with an air of pride, "Well, what do you think?"

The neighbor rubbed his chin and pondered a bit. Then he shifted his chaw of tobacco and said, "Better not sell your mules." (This wasn't one of our nicest neighbors.) But we proved him wrong. Plenty wrong.

We plowed with our tractor. We hauled hay. We did just about anything you can do with a tractor, and I do mean anything. We used that tractor for a long time, and she was one super addition to the family.

Then came the day I'll never forget.

Several of my friends and I asked Dad to take us for a tractor ride down to the river. Of course he agreed. Proudly. So on we jumped. Some on the sides, some on the front, some hanging on back. Me? I stood beside Dad and held onto the seat.

It was one great ride. Until? Until we headed over a steep hill and something broke. Now all of sudden the tractor began to pick up speed.

"Jump," Dad yelled. "We got no brakes." So we jumped. Every one of us totally abandoned ship and landed in the tall sage grass.

When I stood up, I saw Dad still on the tractor. Going like a race car now, he was really moving, bouncing three feet off the rough ground. But he was hanging on, hard. One hand on the steering wheel, the other clutching that seat.

"Jump. Jump!" I yelled at the top of my voice. "Its gonna turn over."

Then came the miracle. Suddenly that runaway darling stopped. She stopped stone cold all by herself. Done roving.

I ran to Dad, who was white as a sheet but still gripping that seat, tight. "Why didn't you jump, Dad? You could of been killed."

"Shut up," he growled. "And help me get my hand loose."

Then I saw it. My poor, ingenious, inventive father had caught his thumb in one of those seat holes.

Of course we did finally set him free, but it wasn't easy. And, believe me, that was the end of it. Nobody in our family and none of our neighbors ever discussed the incident again. Not once. And I do mean *Never*.

Plus nobody ever rode that tractor again.

And I mean "Never" for that statement, too.

I have often wondered, though, whatever happened to that glorious homemade tractor? I suppose if you dragged the river, you might find her rusting away on the bottom.

But I'll tell you a couple things that tractor did for me:

One more time I realized how lucky I was to have a dad like mine. He'd never give up till he tried his best to "make do," as he called it. And that's a good quality for any of us, isn't it?

Then too, when I need a laugh way down inside (and don't we need all of these we can get) I can rely on this one—I just think of that day our homemade tractor almost ran away with my dad caught by a single thumb.

"Coming home from school was big-time expectation. I could smell her peanut butter cookies at least a mile down the road."

Mama's kitchen

MY FAVORITE ROOM IN OUR HOUSE was Mama's kitchen. It must have been hers, too, because she sure spent a lot of time there.

I remember waking up on cold winter mornings. Sticking my head out from under the blanket. Smelling the wonderful aromas.

What aromas?

A big pot of Maxwell House coffee on the back burner. Biscuits baking in the oven. Sawmill gravy in its early stages, simmering in a black iron skillet. A platter of just-fried sausage. When you combine all this with a half-dozen farm-fresh eggs fried over easy, you have one fine country breakfast.

Cholesterol? It hadn't been invented yet.

On cold mornings, I'd get to the kitchen as fast as I could. Mama got up early and had a fire roaring in her stove. It was the only warm room in the house.

If I got there early enough, she'd fix me a cup of cocoa. I'd drag a cane-bottom chair up next to the warm stove. Sip my cocoa and watch her make biscuits.

She'd get a big bowl from the cabinet. Place it under a metal container in the flour bin. Turn the crank. See the flour sift into the bowl?

Then she'd dig a little hole in the flour with her finger. Add a dab of baking soda. (Mama never measured.) Next, drop in some hog lard. Stir while adding buttermilk. Roll the fine dough to a half-inch thickness. Cut it with a biscuit cutter. Now, while they bake, she fries sausage and eggs and stirs the gravy. A breakfast fit for any king.

After breakfast, Mama would wash and dry the dishes. Then she'd wash and iron our clothes. Clean the house, do assorted chores and start supper.

As much as I loved breakfast, supper was my favorite meal. (*Dinner* was our word for the noon meal.) Especially in early spring, it was everybody's favorite.

We'd dig new potatoes. Mama would cook them in cream gravy to go with her big skillet of corn bread.

Lettuce was one of the first things from the new garden. She'd chop new onions – blades, too, on the lettuce and pour in a little hot bacon grease. If you've never had a salad like that, take my word for it—you can't sit still and eat it. It was what Tennessee Ernie Ford used to call "shirt-sleeve eating." Nothing fancy, just plain good!

Eating only got better when summer arrived.

My favorite meal was sliced ripe tomatoes, fried potatoes, fried cabbage, and sweet corn, boiled on the cob. Of course, every meal included corn bread.

Now let me tell you about the desserts. When it came to making sweets, my mama was second to nobody.

Recipes? No, didn't need them. She just seemed to know how to do it.

Coming home from school was big-time expectation. I could smell her peanut butter cookies at least a mile down the road. (Well, yes, that's stretching it a little. But if you'd put your mouth to one of her peanut butter cookies, you'd excuse me for over-enthusiasm.)

How did she do it? She rolled them in little balls, pressed them flat with a fork and made a little checked design on top. Sprinkled a little sugar on, too. Blue ribbon cookies at anybody's state fair.

Dozens of cakes, pies and cobblers. Chocolate and strawberry cream pies were my favorites. But running a close second was a molasses stack cake. The recipe can be traced to the early settlers of this country. Since sugar was sometimes hard to get, molasses was often used as a sweetener.

Do you know how good dried-apple icing can be? Golden brown layers with a molasses flavor. Like the old song goes, "It'd make your eyes light up and your belly say howdy."

Her pies? If she cut each pie into four sections, I usually had two pieces at supper. Then, an hour later, give me another piece or two. You can imagine, Mama's pies didn't last long at our house. It was sorta like we "breathed" them up.

Yet Mama always made only three pies at a time. You wonder why? She had three pie pans, that's why.

Mama still lives in London, Kentucky, so I go see her as often as I can. But I never go without calling. You've already guessed why, haven't you? When I call, I say, "I'm coming to see you tomorrow. I'll be there about dinner time, but don't go to any trouble."

You know what happens, because she's my mama. When I arrive the next day, I'm met with a meal exactly like I remember from childhood.

You know what else I say?

"You shouldn't have gone to this much trouble, Mama." Then I reach for some more corn bread or a piece of that strawberry cream pie.

"As a kid I wore my share of feed-sack shirts. I remember how proud I was of those clothes my mama made."

Saks Fifth Avenue
it wasn't

THE LITTLE GENERAL STORE ON PARKER'S CREEK sold cow and hog feed. Hundred pound sacks. They were made of beautifully printed fabric. The cotton cloth sacks came in all different colors, all kinds of designs. Perfect for making shirts, skirts, dresses, even overalls.

How we loved those sacks!

I don't know who thought up the idea. Feed in material suitable for making clothes was one bright concept, wasn't it? I bet there's been many a cow overfed because some farmer's wife got a little too eager to sew herself a new dress.

I loved Saturday mornings at the Parker's Creek store. Here came the farmers and their wives. In wagons, pickup trucks, old flivver cars. Coming for their week's supplies.

Fashion and style by the hundredweight.

Once I was at an all-day singing and dinner on the grounds of our little church. A long table of food was spread under the shade trees in the side yard.

Two ladies were in polite conversation. Looking good, I might add, in their brand-new feed-sack dresses.

I was dipping up potato salad when I sensed something dreadfully wrong somewhere. One of the good-looking ladies had spotted a woman way down the table wearing a dress made from the same sack-print as the one she was wearing.

What could Lady 1 do? First, she stuck her nose in the air. Then she said, out loud, "Looks like the feed-sack people could sell their patterns one at a time. I hope it looks better on me than it does on her."

As a kid I wore my share of feed-sack shirts. Mama was an excellent seamstress. She made lots of clothes for Dad and me. She also made dresses for herself and Norma Jean. We knew we were fortunate. A lot of people in Appalachia back then didn't even have feed sacks. They couldn't afford store-bought food for their animals.

I remember how proud I was of those clothes my mama made. And today I'm thankful that while she made them, she taught me another lesson. I can still hear her say it.

"IT'S NOT THE SHIRT THAT'S IMPORTANT, CARL. WHAT REALLY MATTERS IS WHAT'S INSIDE THE PERSON WHO'S WEARING IT."

And I've found this is true—no matter if your shirt's from Saks Fifth Avenue or made of sacks from Parker's Creek.

"After supper we'd pop corn, Mama would make a platter of fudge, and here we go. Tune the radio to 'WSM, Nashville, Tennessee, Home of the Grand Ole Opry."

"What'cha got in the sack?"

HERE HE CAME DOWN THE LANE. My dad. Dinner bucket in one hand, sack in the other.

Remember when you were little? Every time your parents carried a certain size sack, you asked, "What'cha got in the sack?"

That's what I said right then.

"What I got," Dad said, "is a little electric radio." White, with two knobs, about the size of a breadbox. There it sat on the little table near our fireplace.

On cold winter evenings, I discovered a wonderful new world: *Fibber McGee and Molly, Our Miss Brooks*, Red Skelton, Burns and Allen.

On Fridays and Saturdays I'd finish my chores early to have more evening. After supper we'd pop corn, Mama would make a platter of fudge, and here we go. Tune the radio to "WSM, Nashville, Tennessee, Home of the *Grand Ole Opry*." Anticipation. Anticipation. Here comes the comedy routine of my favorites, Minnie Pearl and Rod Brasfield.

The first story I remember Minnie telling was about Brother. This was her own great big brother, adult, grown up everywhere except above his ears. But in this story, when they took him to town, everyone thought he had the pox. Why? Because they'd been trying to teach him to eat with a fork. So he'd been stabbing himself here, there and everywhere. How many times did I hear Minnie tell that one over the years? Many, many, and always good for laughs.

Why did so many of the great shows come on in late afternoon, "school's out" time? Seems like they always did. So I'd run all the way home to catch my favorites—Sergeant Preston of the Yukon with his wonder dog, King. Chase those crooks through the wilderness, through the snowstorms, bring 'em to jail. How could Sergeant Preston and King always be on the side of right? Never you mind, they always were.

And didn't you love the Lone Ranger and his sidekick, Tonto? Bank robbers, cattle rustlers and outlaws, they caught 'em all. Here they came, the Lone Ranger and Tonto on their horses, Silver and Scout. Restoring law and order.

Puzzling, wasn't it, that the Lone Ranger wore a mask, and no one ever seemed to notice until the end of the show?

But with favorite shows and favorite people,

everything doesn't need to make sense, does it?

Dad didn't realize it that day, but he was opening up the whole world to his son. Isn't that another thing dads are for?

"Long before the topic was so popular, the people of Appalachia were big on values."

"Do you right and treat you fair"

VALUES ARE HOT COPY THESE DAYS. How long has it been since you've been in a discussion on values?

Politicians talk about values. TV preachers do, too. The media. School teachers. Parents and grandparents. And would you believe what Aunt Clara told me? She said they even got into a brouhaha about values at her bridge club.

Long before the topic was so popular, the people of Appalachia were big on values. They wanted to "do you right and treat you fair." Truthful, honest, hardworking. Lived by the Golden Rule.

Example:

My Uncle Con owned a little general store. His store was on a gravel road next to his farm. Uncle Con grew tobacco, corn and a few whiteface cattle. Plus ponies.

One morning, Uncle Con looked out the

window, and here came Roscoe. Roscoe lived right near five miles away. He was one of several sons who cut timber with their father. They were a hard-working family who kept mostly to themselves. Good, accommodating neighbors. When they did business, you could count on it — always fair.

But this morning, Roscoe wasn't in the store for business. Something more serious was on his mind.

"Morning, Con."

"Morning, Roscoe. What can I do for you this morning?"

"Well, Con, I come to talk with you about something. We been cutting timber over the hill yonder, and we leave our mules out there at night. I nailed a few railings to some trees, and made a little pen for 'em. Then I built a feed box so we can fill it up with corn. But something's been coming and eating our corn. Know what I think? I think some of your ponies are gettin' out, and I think they're gettin' the corn."

"Naw, I doubt it," Uncle Con said. "My fences are too good for that. But if you catch 'em, let me know. We'll put a stop to it."

"OK, Con," Roscoe said as he headed back down the road.

A few days later, Uncle Con looked up and who do you suppose? Roscoe. But not Roscoe like he should have been. This was Roscoe with bloody cuts all over head, arms and neck.

"What in the world happened to you, man?"

Roscoe dropped his head.

"I just come to tell you, Con, I'm sorry I accused your ponies. It wudn't them at all."

"Well, what was it?"

"I went to the woods way before daylight this morning to catch what it was. I put corn in the feed box and sat down behind a tree.

"In a few minutes, I dozed off. When I woke up, I looked around the tree, and I could tell there was something standing at the feed box between my mules.

"In the dark, I thought it was one of your ponies, so I slipped in the pen real slow. Then I grabbed that thing by the tail and hollered real loud.

"But, Con, it wudn't no pony. It was a deer. I don't think anybody had ever grabbed that deer by the tail before. He plain went wild. Pawed me all to pieces. Thought he was goin' to kill me. Knocked me out, and when I come to, he was gone.

"So I just come over here to tell you I'm sorry for accusing your ponies."

Roscoe — bruised, cut, sore and bleeding — had walked five miles to ask Uncle Con's forgiveness.

How far would I walk to apologize to someone I've wronged?

Anyone around here want to go with me?

"Uncle Arlo could stretch the truth to the breaking point."

Uncle Arlo's bottling works

Ever seen a genuine moonshine still in operation?

I have. When I was a boy, moonshiners were plentiful. People accused my Uncle Arlo of practicing the poteen art (whiskey making). I was never sure about that. Aunt Mavis would have cracked his head with a churn dasher if he'd even thought of it. But if he didn't, he'd lie and say he did.

"Yea, used to have a little bottlin' works," he'd laugh and say. "Made a drink called Summer Vacation. After two big glasses, school's out." Uncle Arlo could stretch the truth to the breaking point.

Rumor has it his drink inspired three fellows to play a game. They'd disappear behind the barn and sit in a circle. Pass a half-pint amongst them for about fifteen minutes. Then, one of the three would get up and leave, and the other two had to guess which one it was who left the circle. You get it, don't you? They got in bad shape real fast.

The drink also inspired a rumor that involved one of Uncle Arlo's customers. This fellow bought a quart on Saturday and was never seen again. But his horse came home the following Monday, saddle on backwards.

One story Uncle Arlo liked to tell on himself was about sampling his own wares. That always meant trouble. Once, after a couple of water glasses full, he went to town and rented an empty store "to put in an animal museum." Charged people one quarter to enter and see "the animals and the snakes." Unfortunately, he was the only one seeing them. Naturally, people complained to the sheriff that he was operating under false pretenses.

"The sheriff never did arrest me," he'd say. "Because before he could make an arrest, I gave him a couple of drinks. Then I sold him a half-interest in the store." He'd slap his legs and laugh loud enough to be heard in the next county. My Uncle Arlo, he was a character.

Moonshining is frowned upon by most good

citizens. Some oppose it on moral grounds; others believe it's bad for your health. However, not everyone agrees. Reminds me of a conversation I overheard. Two elderly gentlemen sitting on a bench, discussing the matter.

"I hear the price of likker is going up," one said. His friend, who was known to have a liking for the stuff, said, "Well, I never did think they charged enough."

A moonshiner had to be careful. It was illegal to make whiskey and not pay taxes on it. So government "revenuers," as they were called, were always snooping around.

The revenuers learned to look for certain telltale signs. For example, a little stream of white smoke between two mountains in an isolated area might indicate illegal activity.

They also noticed our habits. Say, one of those long-legged mountaineers arrived at the store in his horse and buggy to pick up a week's supplies. If he ordered a pound of coffee, two pounds of bacon, a dozen eggs and five hundred pounds of sugar, you could bet he wasn't making jelly.

Moonshining flourished during the Great Depression. Not because people thought it was the right thing to do. They knew better. Why then? Many did it to survive. People who wouldn't touch a drop themselves made illegal whiskey and sold it to feed a houseful of hungry children. I guess when your kids are hungry, you'll feed them any way you can.

No, I'm not defending the moonshiners. I'm just telling you they weren't all bad people.

The stills are gone today, and everyone is better off. But back then, they were part of the mountain way of life.

"Mountain logic goes a little beyond common sense. Let's call it common sense with a twist."

Mountain logic

WE ALL KNOW ABOUT COMMON SENSE. But have you ever heard of mountain logic?

Book learning was scarce in our hills. But the common sense we call mountain logic was plentiful.

Some examples...

"Never spit into the wind."

"Don't slap a man if he's chewing tobacco."

"Ain't no use prayin' for rain so long as the wind is blowing out of the east." This doesn't show a lack of faith; it's just practical. Our rains never do come from the east.

See what I mean?

Mountain logic goes a little beyond common sense. Let's call it common sense with a twist.

You want a "for instance?"

My Uncle Jasper knew about mountain logic.

He was a nice man, but something of a loner. Uncle Jasper lived on a hillside farm deep in the holler. His holler was so deep he didn't see many outsiders. Uncle Jasper raised a proud crop of tobacco every year. He also had some hogs and a few head of cattle.

That all made a little money for him. But don't think for a second he'd trust putting any of it in a bank. Not one cent. Never.

Now move closer so you can hear me whisper: "Uncle Jasper kept his money hidden inside a coffee sack. Then he put it under a board in the kitchen floor." Believe me, it was a wad of cash. Fact is, it looked as big as your fist.

One day I asked him about his aversion to banks. "Uncle Jasper, you're losing a bunch of interest the bank would pay you on all that money."

Uncle Jasper laughed.

"I ain't crazy. Every time I put money in my sack, I always put in a little extra — fer the interest."

Here's another example:

A traveling salesman stopped at our little general store for cigarettes. The store owner, an elderly gentleman, started rummaging under the counter. Seems like he took forever. Finally, he brought out a full carton, took out one pack and said, "That'll be twenty-five cents."

"At that price, I'll take the whole carton," the salesman said.

"Nope, can't do that," the old man said. "Jest

one carton to sell. Somebody else might be needin'
cigarettes."

Why would he do that? Just mountain logic.
His regular customers would be along soon.

Cousin Dilbert was a coal miner. For years,
he worked with the same shovel, and did he ever
love it. The handle was a perfect fit for his hands.
The balance so right. Nothing else would do. All
of the miners liked that particular type.

The day came when Uncle Dilbert needed
another shovel. So off he went to the store that
sold 'em.

Owner: "I ain't got no more of them shovels,
ain't gonna get no more."

Cousin Dilbert: "Why not?"

"People bought 'em so fast I just cudn't
keep 'em in stock. So I decided to quit foolin'
with 'em."

Make sense? No. Not to you or me, but to
him pure mountain logic.

Now let me tell you about Bubba. He's my
fishing buddy.

Bubba dreamed of a little getaway place, a
cabin in our mountains. He wanted lots of windows

so he could look out. There's a beautiful lake in the distance.

Now listen to this. He got that mountain house and all those windows. The biggest room was almost all glass. Windows, windows everywhere. If you could stand by his windows, you could sure see Bubba's lake.

Now comes some more mountain logic. Straight from a neighbor who dropped in for a look. Know what he said?

"Shore's mighty smart of you to put in all these lights, 'cause them windows are gonna let in a whole lot of dark."

You wondering again? Me, too. But to the purveyor of this wisdom, plain mountain logic.

Reminds me of the time Cousin Eldean and I fished from early morning to almost dusk. We caught one little fish, eight inches long.

On the way home, Eldean drove and I pondered.

"Eldean," I said, "if you figure all the money we spent today — for the food, our fishing license, the bait, tackle, boat rental, gasoline and everything — that little ole fish cost us about $100 apiece."

Eldean thought a minute. "At that rate," he said, "just be glad we didn't catch two."
Love that mountain logic.

"But what got the riverbank abuzz was the main door. You didn't have to push it or even speak to it. This marvel opened by itself."

The seeing eye door

CAN YOU REMEMBER the first time you heard the word *technology*? I do.

Everybody in our community was excited about this thing called "the seeing eye door."

Kroger built a big, modern supermarket in London, Kentucky. It's the county seat, located seven miles from our home in East Bernstadt.

This new grocery had all the modern conveniences. Carts you could push up wide aisles. A big assortment of fresh produce. Seafood, too. Those shelves were stocked with items we didn't even know existed.

But what got the riverbank abuzz was the main door. You didn't have to push it or even speak to it. This marvel opened by itself.

When word came from town, the skeptical made a special trip just to see it. Others said it must be the work of the devil. Doors weren't supposed to open by themselves. This was unnatural.

135

We'd go to the store just to watch people's reactions. Some caught by surprise were reluctant to dare it. The more adventurous would go in and come out, and do it again. In. Out. They'd shake their heads as if to say, "How does it do that?"

Cletus and I were at the store one Saturday morning when an old pickup rolled onto the parking lot.

A farmer and his wife were in the cab. Back of the truck full. Full of kids. They ranged in size from crumb-crunchers to middle-school age. First, Mama eased out of the cab. Then all those kids piled over the sides and gathered around Mama. Looked like chickens hustling to an old setting hen. Mama's dark-brown coat and red scarf did make her look something like a Rhode Island Red.

Father was a small-framed man who wore a large brown hat. No rooster he. He looked more like a mushroom.

Mama and the kids started toward the store. From her walk, you could tell who was the boss at their house.

Husband lagging behind, they neared the door.

One youngster, a little towheaded boy dressed in bib overalls, started for the door.

Mama must've heard about that door. She yelled and grabbed the little fellow, jerking him back hard enough to give him whiplash.

She yelled to her husband. "Henry, come here!" Henry came. He came like you and I would come for a whipping.

"You go in first," she barked. "We'll foller."

Breathing deeply, Henry straightened his hat and braved the unknown. Courage? Maybe. Maybe anything the door might do to him wouldn't be as bad as disobedience to Mama.

Seeing he was still among the living, Mama and the kids followed.

Technology had come to London, Kentucky.

"'There she is,'Burl said,
as he pointed down a line
of cars to that 1948
humpback Chevrolet.
'Ain't she a beaut? Look
at her paint job. I love
yellow, don't you?'"

The little one-owner

ONE SATURDAY MORNING IN LATE SPRING, Burl and Larvel Atwell stopped by my house. They did that often, but this time it was something special. They were going to town and would I go along?

"I've saved up some money," Burl began, "and I'm gonna buy me a car." He'd just turned sixteen.

We headed out the gravel road to hitch a ride on US 25.

Larvel and I were three years younger than Burl. Just the thought of getting a car gave us chill bumps. The more we talked about Burl's car, the faster we walked.

Burl said his car would have big wide sidewalls, white ones. Fancy hubcaps, too. He might even get mud flaps with little reflectors. "Shore would be glad to have a car like that," Larvel said.

Burl told us when he got his car we'd go into

139

London every Saturday night and just drive around. One weekend we might even go to the Smoky Mountains.

"Gollee," we said. "That's way over in Tennessee."

"Ain't no fur piece if you have a car." (Burl going on.) So we kept walking and talking about seeing the world.

As we approached the highway, I asked, "What happens if we get to town but can't find a car?"

"Don't you worry." (Burl again.) "As a matter of fact, I already got one picked out. Saw it last week. It's a little one-owner, and it'll suit me just fine."

About that time, the Johnsons from down the road came around our curve. Burl stuck out his thumb, and Mr. Johnson slammed on his brake.

"Hop in, boys. Plenty of room." So we scrambled over the cattle racks and Burl thumped the cab top. That was the regular signal to let the driver know we were in. As the truck picked up speed, Larvel's long red hair blew straight back.

"Larvel," Burl kidded, "you look like a mop that's been hung out to dry."

"You better shut yore mouth," Larvel said. "You're getting bugs on your teeth." We all laughed.

As we rolled into London, Burl tapped the cab top again, and Mr. Johnson stopped. Stopped right there at the used-car lot.

"There she is," Burl said, as he pointed down a line of cars to that 1948 humpback Chevrolet. "Ain't she a beaut? Look at her paint job. I love yellow, don't you?"

"Looks like a jonquil in a field of clover," Larvel said, meaning "real yellow."

I thought it looked like a taxi, and as we got closer I knew why. The new paint wasn't thick enough to hide those faint, black letters "T-A-X-I."

"Who owned the car before?" (Me asking.)

"Some company in town." (Burl answering.)

A voice boomed from behind. "Howdy, fellers."

We wheeled around, and there stood a fellow no more than five feet two. About that big around, also. Huge smile across his large round face. Stubby black cigar stuck in his jaw. He wore a brown-striped tie that needed six more inches to reach over his potbelly. Plaid coat that didn't match his tie. Fact is, he looked like Marryin' Sam from the Lil' Abner comics. But never mind style, he made up that lack with personality.

"You was in here last week, wasn't you? (looking at Burl). "Well, like I told you then, this little cream puff is just what you need."

"Doesn't the mileage seem a little high?" (Burl once more.)

"Naw," the salesman reassured him. "A hundred thousand miles is nothin' on a good car like this.

Anyway, look at these tires. Still have lots of tread on 'em. Spare in the trunk, too. This baby has everything. With that heater on any winter day, you'll stop every ten miles to fan yourself. Now look at this radio. One of the finest radios made. Yessirre, this little machine is going to make someone very happy."

Now the salesman glanced at Burl to see if his pitch was working.

"How much do you want for it?" Burl blurted.

The salesman propped one foot on the bumper, looked off into the distance as if pondering and rubbed his chin. "Well, son, I wouldn't do this for just anybody. But you're such a nice boy, I'd like to help you. 'Course I won't be making any money, but I'll let you have this little one-owner for fifty dollars, and that's a steal."

Keep in mind, fifty dollars was a lot more money in those days than it is today.

"I'll take it," Burl said, voice trembling with excitement.

As they walked toward the office to close their deal, we heard the salesman say, "I'm proud of you, son. It warms my heart to help people like you." His smile and tone of voice made me think he might be exaggerating just a little.

When the paperwork was completed, Burl emerged from the office. He was grinning like a mule eating saw briars (that's a real delicacy for mules).

Twirling a keyring on his finger, Burl said,

"She's all mine now. Hop in. Let's take her home and show her off."

Larvel grabbed the front seat. I hopped in back. Burl just sat for a minute. He looked the dashboard over, felt the steering wheel, turned the key and hit the starter.

VAROOOOOOM. The engine settled down to a nice hum. We eased cautiously onto the street and headed north. Burl kept both hands on the wheel. Larvel turned on the radio and hung his right elbow out the window.

By the time we neared East Bernstadt, Burl had more confidence. He'd increased his speed to 60 mph. At 60 mph, you can go from one end of East Bernstadt to the other in 30 seconds. There's a sharp curve at one end of town, and on the outside of that curve is a coal tipple (that's a big funnel for loading coal). The speed limit is 25 mph.

"Slow her down," Larvel yelled. Burl hit the brakes. They started to catch, and then (reach for your Kleenex) those tired old brakes gave way. Where the road curved, we went straight. Loud crash. Sound of metal filling the air.

It was quiet for a few seconds. I slowly pulled myself from the corner where I'd been thrown and looked through the windshield. Everything was black, and I don't mean a little black. The front end of Burl's car had disappeared into a mountain of coal. We were wedged between big wooden pillars, and our two front fenders were missing.

Slowly, we emerged from the car and stood there, estimating the damage.

Burl, ever the optimist, spoke first: "Well, she ain't hurt much." And she wasn't, if you don't count two ruined fenders, two front tires and a few parts "much."

A few weeks and a bunch of dollars later, Burl's little "one-owner" was road ready again.

Great little friend, that yellow beaut. Gave us loads of fun. Took us lots of places. Fact is, she expanded Burl's and his best friends' world tremendously.

"One problem developed, though. It involved Mabel. She was a slightly old lady from down the road, and she shared a party line with us."

Telephones come to the mountains

Do YOU REMEMBER YOUR FIRST TELEPHONE CALL?
I remember mine. I was in the eighth grade.

Uncle Buford and Aunt Patsy had left East
Bernstadt to find work in Ohio. We hadn't seen
them for too long. So a bunch of us decided we'd
go for a visit. One Friday afternoon, we piled in
Uncle Maynard's old Hudson and headed to the
general store.

"Fill 'er up," my uncle said. "We're going to
Ohio to see kinfolks." Destination? Norwood, a
suburb of Cincinnati. We didn't have an exact
address in Norwood; we figured we could find
Uncle Buford and Aunt Patsy anywhere.

Someone once said Norwood should be the
capital of Kentucky. Why? Because it had more
Kentuckians per square foot than any other
place on earth. When good jobs were scarce, as
they usually were, a lot of mountain people
moved to Norwood. Employment was hard to

come by at home.

We topped off the tank and headed north on US 25. It was about a four-hour drive. The Hudson was roomy and gave us a smooth ride. Car packed inside and out; Uncle Fred's suitcase was strapped on top. He'd tied a bushel of potatoes, cabbages and turnips up there, too. For us folks it was only polite to take something when you visit.

As we rolled through the streets of downtown Cincinnati, Cousin Dilbert played "Wildwood Flower" on his flattop guitar. We lowered the windows to get some fresh air. People stared as if they knew we were from out of town. We waved and moved on.

In a few minutes, Uncle Maynard drove into a filling station. "Well, here we are, but we're going to have to call and find out where they live. Does anyone know the number?"

Carl to the rescue. "I do. It's TW1-3097." So Uncle Maynard appointed me to call.

I ran to a phone booth. This was an exciting moment for me. I dropped in a dime and dialed. Something was wrong. The operator came on the line and asked if she could help.

"Yea, if you want to," I answered.

"What's your number?" she asked.

In my best Kentucky mountain accent, I said, "Oh, we ain't got nary number — that's why we're calling from this here phone booth."

The operator laughed. I didn't know why.

Then she said, "No, I mean what's the number of the phone you're calling from?" I gave her the number, but I didn't realize she was putting the call through for me. Uncle Buford answered, "Hello...hello? Hello?"

I turned to Uncle Maynard. "Somebody's already on the line."

Thank heaven, Uncle Buford recognized my voice at that very moment. In the background, a train was blowing its lonesome whistle. (I forgot to tell you the phone booth was right by a railroad track.) Uncle Buford thought someone was crying. "Lord have mercy. Something's bad wrong."

"Ain't nothing wrong," I said.

Then Aunt Patsy took over. "You're here," she said. "Hallelujah. You've come to see us."

Well, we had one fine time in Norwood, Ohio, and I'll never forget: this was the place I made my first telephone call.

Remember yours?

Until I was a junior in high school, the nearest telephone was at the general store. Two miles from our house.

It was one of those wooden-box types. Nothing fancy. Remember?

Most of us didn't know how to use a phone. We'd never talked on one.

149

When we needed to make an emergency call, we'd stop in the store. The store owner gave us telephone instruction.

On this particular day, Eugene asked for help to call his sister in Ohio. (Eugene was a farmer from down river.) Naturally, he was self-conscious. This was his first time, too. To make matters worse, several neighbors were in the store. There they sat on feed sacks stacked near the phone. Just passing the morning, they could hear every word Eugene said.

When Eugene began the call, everyone got real quiet. The store owner, being a little mischievous, said, "Now, you'd better talk real loud 'cause this is a long-distance call. If you don't talk real loud, she won't hear a word you're saying."

Talk loud? Eugene took the store fellow's advice and hollered. Loud. Real loud. All those loafers fell back on the feed sacks laughing louder than Eugene. One of the real cutups yelled (loud), "Eugene, I believe yore sister coulda heard you *without* that telephone."

Finally. Phones were on the way. They already had them in town. Now the Mt. Zion community would be modern, too.

The telephone men came through with chain

saws and axes. They cut a wide swath along every little road and hillside to make room for the wires and poles. A "right-of-way," they called it.

I watched this progress every day from the school bus window. It seemed to take forever. Then one day when I got off the bus and headed down the lane to our house, I saw the new wire. It ran from the pole to our house. I dashed in. There it sat—a black telephone with a rotary dial. Modern. Beautiful. The latest model, right here on our living room table.

"We're on a party line," Mama said.

"What's that?"

"Well, there are four other people on our line, and you can't use the phone if someone else is using theirs," she said.

Before long, we discovered another use for the party line. By listening in on the conversations of the others, you could hear the latest news. Who's in the hospital? Who's visiting from out of town? Who's in trouble with the law? Who's expecting a new baby? All kinds of good stuff.

One problem developed, though. It involved Mabel. She was a slightly old lady from down the road, and she shared a party line with us.

Mabel liked to listen in, but she hadn't quite got the hang of it. Mabel didn't understand that she should wait until someone else was on the line before picking up her receiver. Quietly, so she wouldn't be detected. No, Mabel just kept the receiver to her ear, even when no one else was on the line. She'd sit for hours, as if she were waiting for a fish to bite.

One day Dad had to make a call, but he couldn't get a dial tone. He could hear breathing on the line and figured it must be Mabel. But no matter what Dad said, Mabel didn't utter a word. She sat and listened.

Finally, Dad said, "I sure wish I knew where I could buy three or four dozen good, fresh farm eggs." Without even thinking, Mabel yelled, "I sell eggs."

"Mabel, that you holding up our line?" Dad yelled back.

You can bet that cured our Mabel problem.

For a while!

"On the third night of Cowboy's visit, Grandpa broke into one of those big tales with an invitation."

Ride 'em, cowboy

IF YOUR FAMILY IS LIKE MINE, I bet you've got at least one colorful character who is everybody's favorite.

Mine was Aunt Docita. She was a loving woman, heart of gold, tough as a pine knot. Small, no more than a hundred pounds soaking wet, and a real smoke stack. Three packs of Camels a day. Every day.

But that's not all she did with her spare time.

What she did was to get married. Eight times. Eight husbands. That's right. Eight husbands. Count 'em. Eight.

I never knew most of them. Just heard of them when she'd write. Of course, she and her husbands were the talk of our family reunions.

My favorite was a magician. He could throw his voice, make a broom walk across the floor, even make money disappear. Making money *appear* would have been a better trick in those days.

Then, one day, the magician made himself disappear. Out the door. Vanished. Gone.

Aunt Docita was on the look again.

What she found next was a cowboy. He said he was from somewhere out West, and he had it all. Boots, big hat, leather belt, shiny silver buckle. He even wore spurs, and was I impressed? You bet.

Right after Aunt Docita and Cowboy hooked up, they came to visit. And right away, I noticed something unusual about him. Nobody else got to say much because Aunt Docita's cowboy did all the talking.

After supper, we'd bunch up near the fire and listen to Cowboy's stories. He'd ridden broncos, Brahma bulls, wild ponies. He'd roped steers, throwed 'em down and tied 'em up in record time. That's what he said, and believe me, it was one awesome recitation.

On the third night of Cowboy's visit, Grandpa broke into one of those big tales with an invitation.

"Sounds like you can ride anything. Wanna try my never-been-rid mule? Name's Tobe. If you can break wild horses, you can break a mule, don't you think?"

"Happy to," Cowboy said with a confident swagger.

Next morning, bright and early, there we were, sitting on the corral fence, waiting.

I should tell you, Tobe was one of Grandpa's favorite working team. Jack, the partner mule, was a gentle character. He'd ride four of us kids on his back at the same time. But Tobe was something else. Nobody rode Tobe. And if you tried, he'd pitch you off his back quicker than it took you to get on. This was one mean mule for ridin'.

Now here came Cowboy all dressed up for the occasion. Shiny belt buckle, leather boots, new chaps, classy outfit all the way.

Next on the scene came Grandpa and Tobe headed for Grandpa's tobacco patch. We all followed.

Did you know this about a tobacco patch? When it's just been harvested, there are rows and rows of dried tobacco stalks. Hard, very hard. Each one sticking straight up. Six inches? Maybe more.

"Hope he don't get throwed," someone said. "Could put out an eye. Hurt you real bad."

Then came the big moment. Grandpa's invitation: "I'll hold the bridle while you get on. Then he's all yours."

You can be sure we all backed up to give Tobe and Cowboy plenty of room.

Now watch this. Cowboy grabs Tobe on the mane and pulls himself up. Grandpa gets out of the way. Fast.

For a second or two, Tobe just stands there. That wild look comes into his eyes, and his ears go straight up. One switch of his tail, two switches, three. Then Ole Tobe kicks both hind legs as high as the sky, and off goes Cowboy. Flat on his back, there in the stalks, stone cold.

Is he breathing? "He's okay," Grandpa says. "Stand back. Give him air."

Slowly Cowboy comes to. Grandpa and a couple of my uncles help him to his feet. Then, with one man on each side, Cowboy slowly wobbles back to the house.

What did Cowboy say? Nothing. But Grandpa did. "Wanna try him again tomorrow?" No answer.

When tomorrow came, Cowboy was plumb gone. Left in the night, Aunt Docita with him. We heard later, they headed back out West.

Whatever happened to Cowboy? Nobody ever knew.

Whatever happened to Tobe? Nothing. To his dying day, nobody ever rode him.

Whatever happened to Aunt Docita? She moved to Florida. Died at ninety. A lovable, marrying lady, my Aunt Docita. Loved to visit. But she would never talk about Cowboy. Never.

Yes, she was a real lover, Aunt Docita. Never

knew anybody or anything she didn't love.
Except maybe one mule.

"If the dearly departed was not highly regarded, people just kept their mouths shut. It wasn't nice to speak unkindly of the dead."

"Don't he look natural?"

OUR ANCESTORS came from the British Isles to settle in the Appalachian Mountains. Naturally, they brought many customs with them. One custom, still practiced to a great extent, is "settin' up with the dead." It's somewhat similar to an Irish wake.

When news came that someone had departed, everyone in the community responded. Friends and neighbors went immediately to the home of the deceased. Some stayed around the clock. The family was never left alone until after the body had been interred. That was usually about three days later.

Women in the community started cooking, and soon there was enough food in the house to feed a small army. Those who sat with the dead loved it. It was like a three-day feast.

The body was first taken to the funeral parlor, then brought home. The casket was placed in a prominent spot in the living room (sometimes called the "parlor," for a touch of couth).

Folding chairs, provided by the funeral home people, were placed around the room. They set up extra chairs throughout the house, and even in the yard if it was summer.

As a child, I liked to tune in on the adult conversation.

"Don't he look natural?" (they'd say about almost anyone at any age). "She never had a bad word to say about anybody." "He shore was a good man." (These last two were reserved for the hard-working, regular churchgoers.)

If the dearly departed was not highly regarded, people just kept their mouths shut. It wasn't nice to speak unkindly of the dead.

Lots of people came in the evening after work to show their respect. By nine or ten o'clock, the house and yard were full.

Along about eleven, decisions were made about who'd spend the night. This gave the family a needed rest. By midnight or a little earlier, everyone was gone except for the "settin' up" folks.

When you sat up with the dead, you always stayed in the room with the body. It was never left alone; that would be disrespectful.

One time, Uncle Maynard was settin' up with a neighbor who'd passed on the night before.

Uncle Maynard didn't like settin' up. He said it made him nervous, and he didn't like funerals.

Of course, he knew they were considered great social events.

On this occasion, however, he was caught in a situation where he thought he had to stay. The neighbor he was "settin' up" for had lived in an old, two-story farmhouse. Down the lane from the main road, it looked scary. Even in daylight, it looked scary. There were rumors it had ghosts. The old fellow who'd passed away had sworn he'd seen them real often.

To make matters worse, this was a rainy, dark night, and not many people came. Those who did left early.

Uncle Maynard found himself sitting with the family and only one other neighbor. As the night grew late, the neighbor said, "Y'all go on to bed and git some rest. I'll set up." Uncle Maynard thought it wasn't right to let a neighbor sit alone. He'd stay up, too.

So the family went to bed. Uncle Maynard and the neighbor pulled their chairs next to the big fireplace. Up close like that, they could visit in a low voice. In a few minutes, the neighbor said, "Gonna get me a cup of coffee. You want one?"

When the neighbor went for their coffee, Uncle Maynard studied the room. Flames from the fireplace made little shadows on the wall. Rain beat against the windowpanes. There was no electricity, and the flickering light of kerosene lamps added to the eerie feeling. He was glad the casket was all the way on the other side of the room.

Uncle Maynard thought he was alone, but he wasn't. An elderly gentleman from down the road had come earlier. There he was, over in the dark corner next to the casket. He'd leaned his straight-back chair against the wall and gone sound asleep.

The old man woke up. He peered across the room and saw Uncle Maynard sitting by the fire.

In a sleepy, crackly voice, the old fellow said, "Do ya mind if I smoke?"

Uncle Maynard knocked over three folding chairs as he lunged for the front door. Almost tore the screen off its hinges. Fact is, he near had a seizure.

Setting the coffee cups down, the "settin' up" neighbor ran after Uncle Maynard. In a few minutes, here they came, rain-soaked and cold; Uncle Maynard mighty shaken. As they stood by the fireplace, the elderly gentleman joined them. Silence at first, then the old man said, "Iffen I'd knowed my smokin' was gonna upset you that much, I wud'na even asked."

Right then, Uncle Maynard (addressing no one in particular and everybody in general) said, "I've paid my dues, folks. From now on, somebody else can do the settin' up. I'll still be coming early to pay my respects. Might even have a bite or two. But I'll guarantee you one thing, I'll be getting home before dark."

"We'd sit on the front porch after supper and watch. Those unsuspecting motorists, caught off guard by a car-chasing pig, went plain goofy."

Beware of the hog

THAT'S WHAT THE SIGN SAID, "BEWARE."
And it wasn't a misprint. My buddies Burl and
Larvel had it up in their yard.

They owned a pet pig named Rufus, and
Rufus had a problem. Or should I say, he had
a problem that caused problems if you didn't
know Rufus.

Nobody had ever seen a pig with such a
problem.

Kinfolks, friends, strangers, Rufus ran to greet
them all. And on arrival, he'd rear up on his hind
legs to be petted. So this was the real problem.
Rufus thought he was a dog.

Here's the story.

Burl and Larvel's daddy raised hogs. One
spring, his old sow brought forth her annual litter.
And this little runt pig (later named Rufus) was
among them. Poor runt. Poor Rufus had a hard
time the first few weeks of his life. About half

the size of his brothers and sisters, he was so weak you can guess what happened. At mealtime, he'd get shoved aside from too much competition. To keep their little pig from starving, Burl and Larvel took him from the litter and began feeding him out of a bottle. That's when they officially named him Rufus.

A fun little learner, Rufus took to the bottle quicker than my Uncle Arlo.

Rufus grew like a weed. The boys' mama wouldn't let them keep him inside the house, so they built him a little house of his own. Built in the back yard, it was exactly like a doghouse.

Fact is, they put "Rufus' House" on the front and set it next to the home of Ole Rosie. She was their dad's best coon hound.

Now, it just happened that Rosie had a new litter of pups about then. So it wasn't long until the pups and Rufus were running and playing all over the back yard.

Rosie liked it. She had a free babysitter. Of course, Rosie treated Rufus kindly. Fact is, the boys said she treated everybody and everything so kindly, "she'd think twice before she'd bite a biscuit."

As the pups and the pig grew up together, Rufus tried to do everything the dogs did. When they were big enough to run in the woods, Rufus went with them. Sure, he had trouble keeping up. But the dogs seemed to understand.

Sometimes, they'd even stop and wait.

Did you ever teach a dog how to retrieve sticks?

One day, Larvel and I were in the back yard playing with the pups. That's how you start training a retriever.

So, Larvel would throw a stick. Then, he'd wait for one pup to bring it back. Next, he'd hold that pup and throw the stick to another of the litter.

On one throw, the stick landed right there in front of Rufus. What did he do? He grabbed that stick in his mouth and brought it right back to Larvel.

Larvel patted Rufus on the head with "Good pig, good pig, boy." Rufus seemed to understand that word *good*. Honest, it even looked like he smiled right then.

Before long, Rufus was chasing sticks, playing with rubber balls, burying bones. You may find it hard to believe, but we even thought sometimes Rufus barked.

Well, everything went fine until Rufus and the pups got a year old. That's when they started chasing cars.

Hear that car coming down the road? (Gravel makes a distinctive kind of sound.) So when they heard it, Rufus and the pups would run to the corner of the yard and wait. Then, when the car got closer, they'd tear out after it.

We all had a lot of laughs out of that. We'd sit on the front porch after supper and watch. Those unsuspecting motorists, caught off guard by a car-chasing pig, went plain goofy.

One day, this man had a flat tire in front of Atwells' house. But he wouldn't get out of his car to fix that flat. And you know why? Dogs, he could probably manage, but Rufus?

He propped his feet on the man's rolled up window and stared at him. Crazy, man, crazy. See him wagging his curly little tail? Finally, when the poor, scared driver had honked long enough, we went out and fixed his tire. You'll be interested to know he still wouldn't get out of his car until Burl put a bright-red collar on Rufus and led him back to the yard.

All kinds of people had that same unbelievable pig happening to think about later.

One day, we heard a car horn. In the middle of the road was a lady from our church, a prisoner in her Model A Ford. Rufus was right in front, staring at the radiator, grunting.

"See there," Burl said, "He's trying to bark."

Then came the day when it was time for Rufus to begin living a hog's life. He was plumb too huge for chasing cars and kissing strangers.

Mr. Atwell was real smart, though. He assured us, if we'd let Rufus become a hog again, he would never be sold. We liked that. Rufus would always have a home where we could visit him real often.

The last time I saw Rufus he weighed 500 pounds. Big. King-size. Burl and Larvel and I went one day to his huge pen. There he was, wallering in a nice mud hole.

Of course, I picked up a little stick and said, "Hey, Rufus, fetch this." Then I pitched it out there a ways, but not too far.

What did Rufus do? He raised his head slowly, looked around at me and said (well, all right, maybe I only thought he said), "Can't you see I'm getting too fat to fetch, Carl?" You can bet I was glad he still remembered my name.

There was something new and wistful about Rufus now. Was he perfectly content to be a hog wallering in the mud?

I wonder. Do you suppose there were days when he still thought he was a dog?

"Leroy, who was visiting from Detroit, stood in awe. His mouth hung open. His eyes bugged. He'd been raised in the city. Leroy had never seen anything like this."

"Be sure to leave Cletus at home"

ALMOST ALL THE PEOPLE OF APPALACHIA ARE RELIGIOUS. You'd know that if you saw all the churches of Appalachia. Located every mile or so on the country roads, they dot the landscape.

The names of these churches show the great variety of believers. Baptists, Methodists, Pentecostals, Catholics, independents. Sometimes the name doesn't indicate what kind of church it is. Names like "House of Prayer," "Bob and Betty's House of Worship" and "Dry Branch Tabernacle." Others have more elaborate names such as "The Evangelical Brotherhood of God and Our Lord and Savior Jesus Christ."

Appalachian people have a reputation for being rugged individualists. You'd think so, too, if you knew the diversity and customs of our churches.

One Saturday, word went through our community that a little church five miles back in the hills was having a snake-handling revival. I'd never witnessed one of these services. So, late that afternoon, my buddies Cletus and Bobby Earle and his cousin Leroy and I decided to go. We wanted a firsthand look.

We piled into Cletus' old car and headed out. When we arrived, the church service was well underway. We took the only empty pew, clear in the back. People were standing, singing, and clapping to the music of guitars and tambourines. No one noticed us.

As the service progressed, some worshippers began leaving their pews and stepping up front. Holding their hands in the air, some testified. Some talked in tongues. Others danced and swayed to the music. The entire church was caught up in a frenzy.

Leroy, who was visiting from Detroit, stood in awe. His mouth hung open. His eyes bugged. He'd been raised in the city. Leroy had never seen anything like this.

When the service reached a high pitch, two men carefully lifted a big lard can from the corner. When they set it directly in front of the pulpit, Bobby Earle elbowed Leroy, "Here they come."

One man lifted the lid, and the other reached into the can and pulled out a rattlesnake. Big as a hoe handle. Then he reached back in the can and pulled out another. Holding both snakes over his head for everyone to see, he danced around in a dazed manner. As they say in the mountains, "The spirit was on him."

Then, holding the snakes above him, the man moved down the aisle toward us. Everyone was clapping and singing praises. Cletus, being a little nervous, stepped over the pew and squatted on the floor behind Leroy. When the snake man got to Leroy, Cletus reached under the pew and gave Leroy's leg a hard pinch. Letting out a yelp, Leroy threw up his hands.

Thinking Leroy had gotten the spirit, the snake man thrust those snakes right in Leroy's face. Leroy jumped over the pew, landing on Cletus. They both scrambled for the door. Bobby Earle and me, too, right behind.

As we sped along the gravel road toward home, Leroy piped up, "I shore thought that snake had me by the leg."

I just plain couldn't stand it any longer. "Leroy," I said, "That wasn't no snake. Ole Cletus, he pinched you. Honest, that's all it was."

When Cletus pulled the car into my driveway, I thanked him and, of course, invited them to my church next Sunday.

"No way I'm coming," Leroy said, "Not unless you be sure to leave Cletus at home."

"'Just listen to the music,'Grandpa says. He knows the dogs so well he can tell by the tone of their bark how close they are to the fox."

Sammy Ray, come blow your horn

You've seen the fox hunters on tv, haven't you? Just a little bit, didn't you wish you could have been on one of those horses?

I'm going to tell you about fox hunting, mountain style. No red coats. No riding britches. No black boots, and we didn't blow any trumpet to call the dogs.

Our fox horn was fashioned from a cow horn with a little mouthpiece whittled of wood. Ever think about this? Since the horn is used to call the dogs, why don't they call it a dog horn?

Our fox hunting was always at night. So pretend it's night and come along with me.

Let's go fox hunting with Grandpa. We'll load the dogs and supplies in his old pickup, and away we go to a spot on top of this hill. Grandpa builds a fire. I turn loose the dogs, and we both yell, "Hunt 'em boys. Go get 'em."

Sort of silly, really. They never need even that

177

much encouragement. From the vantage point of the hilltop, hear them? There they go up and down the hills, back and forth across the ridges, down into the hollers. Barks never out of range.

"Just listen to the music," Grandpa says. He knows the dogs so well he can tell by the tone of their bark how close they are to the fox. "Old Blue is looking right at 'im," he says.

It's a couple hours into the hunt now. About nine o'clock, and the fox gets away. The dogs are still hunting, but not barking. Grandpa goes to his truck and brings out a sack stuffed with crackers, baloney, Vienna sausages, potato chips and "Co-colas." Here we sit, eating, looking into the fire. Get it? Fox hunting is just another excuse to be in the woods, build a fire and have an all-night picnic.

Know what else I've heard? I've heard some hunters take along a jug of "corn squeezings." Some call it mountain dew. This could explain why the dogs sometimes get home before the hunters.

As much as Grandpa loved to hunt, he wasn't as fanatic about it as my friends Eudell and Sammy Ray. As grown men, they hunted together for years.

One day, Eudell took sick and was rushed to the hospital. The doctors said he might not make it. Eudell must have sensed that, so he summoned Sammy Ray.

"Sammy," he began, "Do me a favor. May sound a touch odd, but if I die, at my funeral when the preacher's done, I want you to go to the front of the church and blow yore fox horn one more time. It'd make me awful happy."

"I'll do it," Sammy promised.

On the day of the funeral, Sammy Ray was nervous, but not too nervous. He was determined to keep his promise. There he was with his horn heading for the church. Shy as he was, he'd never been before an audience of any kind. But he managed. On his way, he stopped by one of the local "merchants" for a half pint of tonic. That particular tonic was known to wipe away all fears, and it did. By the time Sammy Ray reached the church, his confidence was bulletproof.

So he slipped in the church and took a seat on the back row. Waited. When the preacher finished, Sammy Ray ran to the front, stood by the coffin, popped the fox horn to his lips and let out three long, loud blasts. TOOOOOT. TOOOOOT. TOOOOOT. Then he "called the dogs" by barking like a hound. The congregation looked stunned.

The minister jumped to his feet, grabbed Sammy Ray by the arm and let him have it.

"What in the world are you doing? You CRAZY???"

"Well," Sammy Ray replied. "Eudell asked me to blow this here horn just once more for him."

"I know your friend Eudell," the preacher said, "but *his* funeral ain't til four o'clock."

"The practice game started. Remember, I'd never played in a football game. Never even seen one."

Football comes to Hazel Green

HAZEL GREEN HIGH. Freshman year. Principal steps into our world history class. Announcement: "We're going to have a football team. How many of you guys want to play?"

Hands shoot up. I look at Cletus. He nods, and two more hands go up. Slowly.

Problem?

We didn't know thing one about football. Hazel Green had never had a team. I always wanted to be in sports, but I wasn't coordinated. Too short for basketball.

Baseball? I couldn't hit. Struck out all the time. Another minor difficulty...I couldn't catch the ball. What's left for not being able to do?

Track was another matter. I was a fairly good runner, up to a point. Coach called me his "miler and half-miler." Why? Because I'd start running the mile, and make it half way.

By this time, I'd come to realize Carl would

probably never be inducted into the Sports Hall of Fame.

But there was hope for me in the game of football.

We were to meet the next afternoon. We'd practice behind the school building on a flat area where coal had been mined. The ground was smooth now, but there wasn't one blade of grass. Nothing but hard clay and a thin layer of tiny rocks. Real sharp rocks. How would we know football fields were supposed to be covered in grass?

Big decisions ahead. Who's going to play which position? I could hear the coaches talking that over.

"Now, there's Hurley," one said. "He weighs somewhere near 145, and he can run. Probably good at carrying the ball." (Shows just how wrong a person can be.)

The practice game started. Remember, I'd never played in a football game. Never even seen one.

Center snaps ball. Quarterback hands ball to me.

I head to the right, fast as I can go. At the line of scrimmage: WHAM! I'm hit from four directions. Other team gets ball. There I lay on those tiny, sharp rocks.

I'm thinking, "Must be the ball that's causing the problem."

Coach runs onto field. Checks me out: Am I

still alive? "Get down, get down!" I yell.

Coach: "Why?"

Me: "They may come back."

Two weeks later.

Coach reassigns me to the offensive line. Good. No more carrying the ball. I didn't want to even be NEAR the ball again.

Next big game.

Our team fumbles. What do I do? I stand, staring at the ball.

Teammate yells: "Pick it up! Pick it up!"

Me: "You pick it up. You dropped it."

Time for another change.

Now I become a defensive center.

Coach: "All you got to do is line up and watch the ball. When the center moves it, your job is to hit him as hard as you can."

"Great," I'm thinking. "This I can do."

But there's still one problem.

Our team was the Hazel Green Bullfrogs.

"Killer frogs," to be exact. Meditate a bit now on that name and the teams we were playing. Frogs playing teams named Lions, Tigers, Bears. Even if we yelled "ribbet, ribbet" as loud as we could, who would it scare?

No, I never went to college on a football scholarship. Somehow, I could never get meaner than a frog.

"I stood and waved as the station wagon pulled away, and my family waved back to me. That's one goodbye I'll never forget."

Forty Holsteins and a cap and gown

L̶ONG BEFORE I GRADUATED FROM HIGH SCHOOL, I decided I was going to college. I didn't know how this could possibly happen. No one in my family had ever gone. Times were tough and money was scarce, but I'd managed to save $50.

When we learned that tuition for the summer term was $37.50, Dad slapped me on the back and said, "Well, son, you'll have enough money left over to buy a book." (He was serious.)

Then, two weeks before my graduation from high school, I received a telephone call. It was from a professor of agriculture at Eastern Kentucky State College in Richmond. I felt big-time getting a call like that.

Professor Taylor had grown up in our community and was a friend of the family. His mother had been one of my good teachers at Mt. Zion Elementary. That's how he knew I wanted to attend college. And most likely how he knew I didn't have much money.

Part of Professor Taylor's duty at Eastern was to manage the college dairy farm. It was run by four students, and two of them were graduating. Was I ever thrilled when he offered me a job!

The job meant I'd get up every morning at four. I would help milk forty Holsteins and deliver the pasteurized milk to the dorms and cafeteria. Then, we'd milk again in the afternoon. Since this job was my opportunity to go to school, I wasn't bothered by the work or the demanding schedule.

Before we continue, I should tell you I'd milked most of my life. We had one cow, Ole Nell. She was half white-face and half Jersey, and I milked her by hand in a #4 lard bucket.

High school graduation was on Friday, June 7, and this summer I wouldn't be playing around any. The new job started immediately. Four o'clock that coming Sunday afternoon, I'd report. Two days to get ready.

Sunday morning, we attended church and had a big meal at Grandma's house. Then, my mama and dad, sister and Uncle Jim loaded me and one suitcase into our 1957 Ford station wagon.

We headed north on US 25. Richmond was only 50 miles up the road. Yet, as we drove through the little towns on the curvy highway, I had these questions in my mind: "Isn't every mile taking me farther and farther from home?" "Am I leaving home for good?"

Arriving on campus, we passed stately buildings and beautiful old trees that lined the streets. A tingle of excitement ran up my spine. I felt very fortunate to be going to college.

Our destination was a little, brown-brick building located on the edge of campus, next to the dairy barn. This would be my new home. Many years earlier, it had served as slave quarters. (My roommates told me later, tongue in cheek, that nothing much had changed.)

Professor Taylor and my roommates were there to greet us. One roommate was my first cousin from another county. He'd gotten the other barn job, so we'd work together.

The two other boys would be living with us. Jim, tall and lanky, was from Wolfe County. Don, more than six feet tall, was as strong as an ox. He was from Jackson County. They both loved to laugh, so I knew at once we'd hit it off real fine.

After the manager showed us around the farm, it was time for goodbyes. I stood and waved as the station wagon pulled away, and my family waved back to me. That's one goodbye I'll never forget.

"Come on, fellows, it's milking time," Professor Taylor called. "Let's go to the barn and get you new boys broken in."

187

That first afternoon, we strolled up the hill to the big, white barn. Don threw open the door, and I could hardly believe my eyes. There were Holsteins as far as the eye could see. I'd never seen cows that big or that many in one place.

"Lord have mercy," I yelled, "what are we gonna do with all these cows?"

"We're gonna milk 'em," Don said.

"Where in the world are we gonna get a lard bucket that big?" I asked. Don laughed and pointed to a large, shiny can. Four black hoses came out the top, and there were suction cups on the end of each hose. I'd never seen electric milkers. When he slapped that contraption on the cow, I jumped back and hollered, "Look there, he's gonna jump-start that Holstein."

My friends never forgot that silly comment, but honest, that's exactly what it looked like to me.

So, maybe it was silly, but I didn't care. It was a great way to jump-start my education. I shall always be grateful to those forty Holsteins.

And grateful, too, for having learned at an early age that life's real riches can't be measured in dollars and cents. We weren't poor–we just didn't have any money.

Acknowledgments

Success doesn't happen because of the efforts of one person. That's especially true with the completion of this book. Several people deserve special recognition:

Michael A. McKinney, president of McKinney Associates, Inc., in Louisville, Kentucky. Mike is my manager, agent and friend. Without his assistance, encouragement and suggestions, I'd still be saying, "Someday, I'm gonna write a book."

Dr. Charlie Shedd, minister, speaker and best-selling author. Two of Charlie's books, *Letters to Karen* and *Letters to Philip*, have sold in the millions. (His newest books, *Brush of an Angel's Wing* and *What Children Tell Me About Angels* [Servant Publications] lead the pack on this theme.) What a gifted writer and teacher! Charlie's insight and wisdom were enormously helpful. I'm honored he likes my humor.

Francis "Doc" Heatherley, publishing consultant. When we had a question, this "doc" had an answer. Francis gave shape, focus and direction to this book. He also favored us with this advice: "Every writer needs an editor. Get Connie Giles to help you. She's the best." We followed Doc's suggestion. Connie graciously agreed. Francis was right — Connie is the best!

More "kudos" to...Mike King, president of King Graphics, and his enthusiastic assistant, JoAnn Bohannon; Roger Fristoe, writer and friend, who loves Appalachia and the ways of its people; Zana Naake, talented photographer whose joyous nature makes *me* laugh; and Janet and Jim Rittenhouse for their valuable assistance and support at our office.

Finally, my family: wife, Angela, and best kids, Lori and Chad. They patiently listen to my stories. They inspire me in ways big and small. They encourage me to follow my dreams. They help me stay on track as I "look for the humor in life." A whole family of cheerleaders. Isn't that nice?

To all of you, my heartfelt thanks.

Carl Hurley

CARL HURLEY grew up in the Appalachian Mountains of Kentucky, in a two-room cabin built by his father. Carl earned degrees at Eastern Kentucky University (EKU) and a doctorate in education from the University of Missouri-Columbia.

For eight years, Hurley was a popular professor at EKU. He resigned in 1982 to pursue his dream of becoming a full-time entertainer. His comedy recordings have created a legion of fans coast to coast. And he's a popular platform speaker, seminar leader and entertainer.

Whether looking at how our lives change (a favorite topic) or taking us back to our roots (wherever they may be), Carl mixes a simple little professorial lesson in with the fun—*humor is good for us!*

"Everyone needs to laugh," Carl believes, and his goal is to share the humor he finds in everyday situations, in our families and in ourselves.

Carl and his wife, Angela, live in Lexington, Kentucky. They have two grown children, Lori and Chad.

The comedy of Carl Hurley

If you like to laugh, you'll enjoy these outstanding comedy recordings by Carl Hurley.

CASSETTE TAPES

Makin' Change
Looking for the Humor
Live from London
Back Home
Live at Renfro Valley
Cavalcade of Comedy
Country Formal
On A Clear Day You Can See Tomorrow (motivational)

VIDEOS

Looking for the Humor
Live at Renfro Valley
Country Formal

To order cassettes, videos or additional copies of this book, or for information about scheduling Dr. Hurley for an appearance, contact:

McKinney Associates, Inc.
PO Box 5162
Louisville, KY 40255-0162
502/583-8222